Who's Endangered on Noah's Ark?

WHO'S ENDANGERED ON NOAH'S ARK?

Literary and Scientific Activities for Teachers and Parents

Glenn McGlathery
University of Colorado at Denver

Norma J. Livo
University of Colorado at Denver

Illustrated by
David Stallings

1992
Teacher Ideas Press
A Division of
Libraries Unlimited, Inc.
Englewood, Colorado

To Sean, Stephen, Dylan, and Kelsey with love and hope that their lives will continue to be enriched by the presence in nature of wondrous beasts of infinite variety.

—GEM

To Emily. —NJL

⚜ ⚜ ⚜

TEACHER IDEAS PRESS
A Division of
Libraries Unlimited, Inc.
P.O. Box 6633
Englewood, CO 80155-6633

Library of Congress Cataloging-in-Publication Data

McGlathery, Glenn, 1934-
    Who's endangered on Noah's ark? : literary and scientific
activities for teachers and parents / Glenn McGlathery, Norma J.
Livo ; illustrated by David Stallings.
    xix, 173 p. 22x28 cm.
    Includes bibliographical references and index.
    ISBN 0-87287-949-6
    1. Endangered species. 2. Zoology--Study and teaching--Activity
programs. I. Livo, Norma J., 1929-   . II. Title.
QL82.M38   1992
591.52'9--dc20   92-19570
                                                              CIP

Contents

Preface

God said unto Noah, "The end of all flesh is come before me; for the earth is filled with violence through them; and, behold, I will destroy them with the earth.

"Make thee an ark of gopher wood; rooms shalt thou make in the ark, and shalt pitch it within and without with pitch.

"And this is the fashion which thou shalt make it of. The length of the ark shall be three hundred cubits, and the breadth of it fifty cubits, and the height of it thirty cubits.

"A window shalt thou make to the ark, and in a cubit shalt thou finish it above; and the door of the ark shalt thou set in the side thereof; with lower, second, and third stories shalt thou make it.

"And, behold, I, even I, do bring a flood of waters upon the earth, to destroy all flesh, wherein is the breath of life, from under heaven; and every thing that is in the earth shall die.

"But with thee will I establish my covenant; and thou shalt come into the ark, thou, and thy sons, and thy wife, and thy sons' wives with thee.

"And of every living thing of all flesh, two of every sort shalt thou bring into the ark, to keep them alive with thee; they shall be male and female.

"Of fowls after their kind, and of cattle after their kind, of every creeping thing of the earth after his kind; two of every sort shall come unto thee, to keep them alive.

"And take thou unto thee of all food that is eaten, and thou shalt gather it to thee; and it shall be food for thee, and for them."

Thus did Noah; according to all that God commanded him, so did he.

—Genesis 6:13-22

This story is the prelude to the tale of the massive flood that was said to have covered the earth, killing every living thing that was not in Noah's ark. The humans and animals that emerged from the ark, according to this story, are the progenitors of all things that are alive today. In a sense, all the humans and animals on earth today can be considered survivors of Noah's ark. However, when the ark docked, after the flood waters subsided, and the animals began to make their own ways in the world, away from the watchful eyes of Noah and his direct care, problems began to arise. Some animals have not fared well, either becoming extinct or near-extinct.

Who is endangered on Noah's ark? Of the former passengers of the ark, which animals are now having trouble surviving? This book introduces a few species that are threatened with extinction.

When Emily, a four-year-old, was asked, "What does extinct mean?" her poignant reply was, "When you don't believe in something, it becomes extinct." Individuals and whole cultures have "believed" in and lived in harmony with the earth and the animals on it. In a letter to President Franklin Pierce in 1855, Chief Seattle of the Dwamish tribe of Washington Territory contrasted the views of the "civilized" white man and the "savage" red man:

We know that the white man does not understand our ways. One portion of the land is the same to him as the next, for he is a stranger who comes in the night and takes from the land whatever he needs. The earth is not his brother, but his enemy, and when he has conquered it, he moves on. He leaves his fathers' graves, and his children's birthright is forgotten. The sight of your cities pains the eyes of the red man. But perhaps it is because the red man is a savage and does not understand.

There is no quiet place in the white man's cities. No place to hear the leaves of spring or the rustle of insect's wings. But perhaps because I am a savage and do not understand, the clatter only seems to insult the ears. The Indian prefers the soft sound of the wind darting over the face of the pond, the smell of the wind itself cleansed by a mid-day rain, or scented with a pinon pine. The air is precious to the red man. For all things share the same breath—the beasts, the trees, the man. Like a man dying for many days, he is numb to the stench.

What is man without the beasts? If all the beasts were gone, men would die from great loneliness of spirit, for whatever happens to the beasts, also happens to man. All things are connected. Whatever befalls the earth befalls the sons of the earth.

It matters little where we pass the rest of our days; they are not many. A few more hours, a few more winters, and none of the children of the great tribes that once lived on this earth, or that roamed in small bands in the woods, will be left to mourn the graves of a people once as powerful and hopeful as yours.

The whites, too, shall pass—perhaps sooner than other tribes. Continue to contaminate your bed, and you will one night suffocate in your own waste. When the buffalo are all slaughtered, the wild horses all tamed, the secret corners of the forest heavy with the scent of many men, and the view of the ripe hills blotted by talking wires, where is the thicket? Gone. Where is the eagle? Gone. And what is to say goodby to the swift and the hunt, the end of living and the beginning of survival? We might understand if we knew what it was that the white man dreams, what he describes to his children on the long winter nights, what visions he burns into their minds, so they will wish for tomorrow. But we are savages. The white man's dreams are hidden from us.[1]

In the past few decades, awareness of and concern for threatened animals have grown tremendously, not only in the United States but worldwide. With enough of this burgeoning "belief," maybe fewer animals will become extinct.

These pages include some of the success stories in conservation. We cannot be sure of the eventual outcome of all these conservation efforts, but we know that we are making strides toward reestablishment of at least a few species. Nevertheless, tens of thousands of other animals and plants have no champions—they will become extinct. The *last* individuals of some species died while you read this. In so many ways we have squandered our inheritance. We have not only not believed in species, we have actively killed them through carelessness and neglect. Although animals did flourish and die out without human intervention, extinction rates have multiplied tremendously since our species made its entrance.[2]

Perhaps future generations will care more than past generations have. Perhaps from the ranks of the careless and callous *Homo sapiens* will arise champions of doomed species who will not only believe but will lead others to believe. That is our hope.

HOW TO USE THIS BOOK

This book concerns ten of the animals that are or have been threatened: wolves, bears, elephants, tigers, leopards, California condors, northern spotted owls, bald eagles, whooping cranes, and alligators. Each section includes a folktale and folklore about the animal and a discussion of its description, behavior, habitat, historic range, current distribution, and status as an endangered species. This section is followed by activities investigating the animal's environment and current status, plus activities involving art, literature, writing, and drama. A bibliography for additional information and reading is included at the end of each chapter.

Who's Endangered on Noah's Ark? is intended for use by children independently, classroom teachers, librarians, and parents of children of all ages. The folktales that introduce each chapter are drawn from many different cultures and traditions. Ideally, they should be read aloud, whether by a teacher or students, so they can be experienced within the oral storytelling tradition from which they come. Teachers can also assign the folktales and background information for individual reading. The activities are brief suggestions to get readers thinking further about the animal. In the classroom, students could work individually or in small groups on one or more of the activities, perhaps choosing one or more from the different sections and sharing their work with the class. Teachers, librarians, parents, and children should think of ways to adapt the activities and should be encouraged to devise their own investigations or extensions.

Integrating Content in the Curricula

A venerable rabbi was deep in discussion with other learned men. The question they were addressing was, "Which is more important—learning or action?" The respected rabbi and another sage argued their points. The rabbi said, "Action is the most important. What use can there be to fine words and eloquent speeches unless they are put into practice?"

The scholar with the opposing view felt that learning was more important. Eventually the wise men concluded that both were right and that "Learning is more important when it leads to action."

—Jewish folklore

Once upon a _____, a very fierce _____ was in great _____. No
one knew how to _____ it because no one _____ knew it was there.
The _____ came quite _____ and that is why today there are no
_____ about this very fierce _____.

There are pieces missing from this short story. Without all the pieces, we can only guess at the meaning and message that the writer or teller intended. Education is much like this when the curricula content areas are treated as separate, isolated material for the learner.

We know several things about learning: They include:

- The learner must be purposefully involved for learning to take place

- Children are very active learners

- Learning builds on experiences and knowledge the learner already has

- The learner needs experiences and interaction with material to develop abstract notions and concepts

- Learning is holistic.

If students are to learn about themselves and their world, and how they are a meaningful part of it all, content materials must be integrated instead of taught in isolation. This means that literature, science, mathematics, social studies, reading, writing, art, and music should all be taught together rather than in isolated chunks. Integrating learning answers the question, "How are these ideas related?" By providing a theme for students to explore, the teacher promotes a sense of connection and continuity among learning activities.

Within the framework of this book, students have some freedom to choose reading materials and help create activities, but are also given a sense of direction for their studies. Students will exercise diverse forms of creativity through readings, discussions, and activities aimed at helping them discover and explore their own talents and abilities. The structure provided must be flexible. Students will need adequate time to complete readings, discussions, and projects. Time must also be alloted for group and individual responses and reflection. The range of possibilities for the students in their work allows them to select issues and topics of personal interest.

Even though there are opportunities for diversity, this book's material still fits in a cohesive framework that includes functional use of information. Reference materials also include other persons and the environment around the learners; printed materials will not provide all the answers. As a start, many suggested activities include invited speakers, field trips, and interviews. Learners must recognize that information is not confined to books, magazines, newspapers, and classrooms. The world around them is also a source and must be invited into the learning process.

Research identifies many activities positively related to increased learning. Discussion of the meanings of stories and articles, both before and after they are read or heard, has a positive relation to learning. Art and music activities contribute to aesthetic and emotional extensions of a theme. Writing and sharing what is read and written further extends personal growth, as does the making of craft and art projects, hands-on experiences, and field observations.

Specific to the topic of this book, endangered species, the whole world of thinkers is essential to solving future problems. That includes biologists, environmentalists, theologians, economists, historians, government agencies, and representatives of industry. All these disciplines must participate in decision making. As we work with learners, we must keep this broad viewpoint in mind. For instance, a government committee of political appointees has the power to exempt species from the protection of the Endangered Species Act when humankind's economic interests so dictate. This committee is commonly known as the "God Squad." It has been compared to Noah standing on the gangplank to the ark, reviewing the species of the world pair by pair, deciding on a purely economic basis which creatures to save and which to consign to extinction. So, as we discuss integration of learning from an academic stance, we must also extend our thinking to look at these issues as if we were biologists, environmentalists, theologians, historians, and representatives of industry and governmental agencies, as well as citizens of the world.

Organizing for Integrated Learning

A variety of strategies can be used to integrate the curricula. They include webbing, mapping, clustering, advance organizers, relationships, flowcharts, and schema. They all include starting with the topic and grouping activities, materials, and ideas related to the topic. Here are samples of webs that generate activities for investigating the topics of "Endangered Species" (fig. I.1) and "Wolves" (fig. I.2, page xvi).

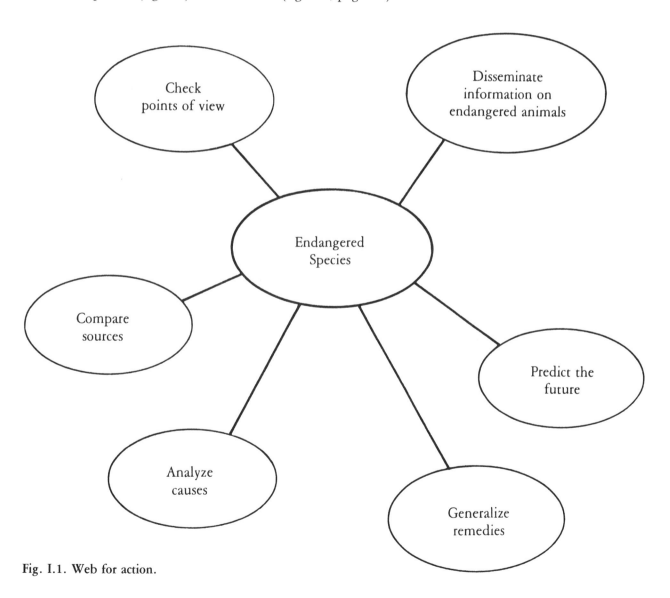

Fig. I.1. Web for action.

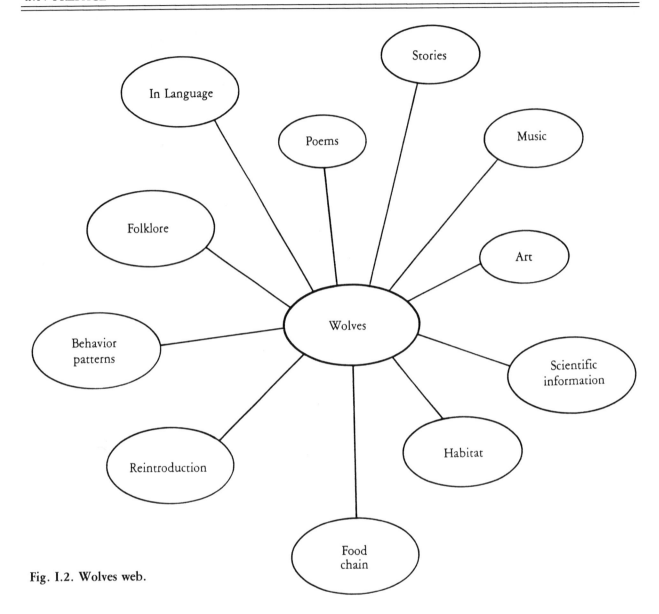

Fig. I.2. Wolves web.

With this skeleton for study, students and their teachers can brainstorm activities to answer the questions they want to explore. They can also develop more specific clusters of topics and ideas for study. Of course they can collect statistics, analyze data, collect materials, invite a variety of speakers to class, and conduct surveys. They can draw, compose, sing, act out, debate, write, read, and create action plans. Learners will be able to select their preferred directions of study and share and present what they have learned with each other.

When hands-on and thinking skills are emphasized, learners profit. The following activities support the language arts:

- Discussing the meanings of stories, both before and after they are read

- Storytelling by both children and adults

- Integrating art activities that relate to what is read

- Encouraging children to read to each other

- Frequently using children's literature in the instructional setting

- Reading to children regularly

- Encouraging children to keep records and write books

- Acting out and debating stories and topics.

These activities truly combine listening, speaking, reading, and writing in an integrated manner that provides individual choices and decision-making skills. Creativity and thinking must be part of each child's learning experience.

This proposed learning plan ensures adaptability and flexibility, experiences in problem solving, and, finally, a varied point-of-view look at each topic. The ultimate evaluation of success might be to refer back to the Jewish story that states, "Learning is more important when it leads to action."

NOTES

1.   Peter Nabokov, ed., *Native American Testimony: An Anthology of Indian and White Relations from Encounter to Disposition* (New York: Thomas Y. Crowell, 1978), 107-9.

2.   William F. Allman and Joannie M. Schrof, "Can They Be Saved?" *U.S. News and World Report* 107 (October 2, 1989): 107.

SUGGESTED READING

Day, David. *Noah's Choice: True Stories of Extinction and Survival*. New York: Viking Penguin, 1990.
    Day recounts extinct animals and tells about some rare ones. Illustrations are by Mick Loates.

DeBlieu, Jan. *Meant to Be Wild: The Struggle to Save Endangered Species through Captive Breeding*. Golden, Colo.: Fulcrum Press, 1991.
    The conservation of endangered North American species through captive breeding and reintroduction to the wild is discussed.

IUCN Conservation Monitoring Centre. *1986 IUCN Red List of Threatened Animals*. Gland, Switzerland: International Union for Conservation of Nature and Natural Resources, 1986.
    This government publication of the Global Environment Monitoring System (GEMS) includes a listing of threatened animals. An extensive index and bibliography make this volume valuable for the researcher.

Rice, Paul, and Peter Mayle. *As Dead as a Dodo*. Boston: D. R. Godine, 1981.
    This book, illustrated by Shawn Rice, describes sixteen extinct animals and suggests the reasons for their extinction. Also discussed is the plight of several endangered animals and the apparent lack of concern people have about these animals and their environment.

Van Allsburg, Chris. *Just a Dread*. Boston: Houghton Mifflin, 1990.
   This story for young readers looks at a dream by the main character in which the earth's future is shattered by pollution. The lesson is that we need to pay more attention to care of the environment.

Van Matre, Steve, and Bill Weiler. *The Earth Speaks*. Warrenville, Ill.: Institute for Earth Education, 1983.
   Many voices are captured in the words and images in this collection of writings by naturalists, poets, scientists, philosophers, and ordinary people. These selections generate both feelings toward and understandings of the natural world.

𝒜cknowledgment

We acknowledge great help in the writing of this book. Thanks to the librarians who have made our research easier. Thanks to our students who give us inspiration and ideas. Thanks, especially, to our spouses; to George, whose gentle humor and wide understanding of practically everything keeps us entertained and informed; and to Debby, who enriches our lives always, all ways.

The illustrations in this book are by David Stallings. The masks were designed by Melanie Penry Mitchell. The photographs of the finished masks on pages 20 and 110 were provided by Deborah McGlathery. The maps were drawn by Pat Martin. We thank them all for their contributions to the book.

Introduction

Don't it always seem to go
That you don't know what you've got 'til it's gone?
They paved paradise and put up a parking lot.
—Joni Mitchell, "Big Yellow Taxi" *

WHAT IS EXTINCTION?

Extinction is forever. Animals that are extinct will never again be seen as living organisms: not in the wild, not in zoos, not anywhere. When the last of a species dies, that species will afterward be found only in the fossil record, in an artistic depiction, or in model form. Examples of extinct animals include all dinosaurs, from the tiniest lizard-like creeper to the giant *Diplodocus*, a multi-ton herbivore of the Jurassic period. Other extinct animals include the woolly mammoth, the saber-toothed tiger, the dodo, the passenger pigeon, and so on. Many of these extinctions occurred before the advent of humans (dinosaurs, for example), so we cannot take the blame for these animals' demise, but others (the passenger pigeon, for example) are recent additions to the list of former inhabitants of earth, for which humans are almost entirely responsible. This book does not elaborate on extinct species, though. Its focus is on some of the many animals that are currently threatened or severely endangered.

Threatened is legally defined in the Endangered Species Act of 1973 as amended as "any species which is likely to become an endangered species within the foreseeable future throughout all or a significant portion of its range." *Endangered* refers to "any species which is in danger of extinction throughout all or a significant portion of its range."

PROTECTION FOR ENDANGERED SPECIES

What can be done about the rising number of threatened and endangered species? The following statistics are sobering, even alarming:

- More than 90 percent of the species that have ever existed are gone.

- As many as 6,000 of the earth's species vanish each year from deforestation alone.

*"Big Yellow Taxi" (Joni Mitchell) © 1970, 1974 SIQUOMB PUBLISHING CORP. All Rights Reserved. Used by permission.

- Tropical forests, under heavy pressure from clearing and development, are home to 50 to 80 percent of the world's species.

- Although many species became extinct before humans appeared on the earth, the extinction rate has risen by a factor of 10,000 since *Homo sapiens* appeared.[1]

- More than 4,000 species are considered threatened.[2]

Many issues surround the saving of various species. Whether you are a child, an adult, a parent, a politician, or a citizen, you will have decisions to make and be affected by the ones society as a whole makes. First of all, the ethical problem of vanishing species must be addressed. Humans share some of the blame for the threatened or endangered status and even extinction of several animal species. It would seem, therefore, that humans owe something to the solution of these problems. The first decision, then, is whether to accept some of the responsibility for species other than our own. The second concerns what, when, and how much to help.

The Ethical Struggle

One can see that, although some plans have been made and even funded to help threatened wildlife, those plans are somewhat erratic. A deeper philosophical issue is whether the American public is ready to save endangered species. The prospect of spending money to save a small fish—the little-known snail darter, for example—while stopping the construction of a dam makes some people bristle. Critics suggest that the money could be better spent by building the dam, thereby bringing jobs and services to people. Issues surrounding endangered species often bring proponents of development into conflict with conservationists. We read about these arguments almost daily in our newspapers and magazines as we, for example, contemplate saving the spotted owl at the expense of the logging industry. Questions concerning endangered wildlife are not easy. There are cogent arguments on both sides of both issues, as students who attempt the activities suggested in this book will soon discover. Only a literate and educated public can make decisions that balance the needs of threatened and endangered wildlife with the needs of a growing society.

Which Species Should Be Helped?

If we as a society decide that it is the responsibility of humans to help the recovery of threatened and endangered species, the next decision concerns just which species need help. In the United States, the Endangered Species Act of 1974 gives the responsibility for developing plans to aid all endangered U.S. species to two federal agencies, the Fish and Wildlife Service (FWS) of the Department of the Interior and the National Marine Fisheries Service (NMFS) of the Department of Commerce. While it is not possible to save all species that are currently threatened with extinction, scientists estimate that almost 70 percent of the domestic species could possibly be helped with appropriate recovery plans. However, by 1988, no recovery plans had been made for 113 species, over 25 percent of those listed at that time.

Both agencies are strapped for funds and are seriously understaffed for the task of helping some 4,600 species proposed for listing. The FWS estimates that about 1,000 of these species warrant immediate protection, but, under its current budget, it can list only about 60 species a year. Estimates are that the most endangered may await federal protection for at least sixteen years. Since time and money are short, it makes sense that the agencies should adopt a triage system (a system that sets priorities for listing). The NMFS has no such system. Although the FWS has a triage system, the General Accounting Office found that the FWS generally ignored the species highest on the priority list and chose to direct its efforts to helping species that have high "public appeal" or seem most likely to bring immediate and visible success. For example, the FWS allocated 25 percent of all recovery funds to just four animals: the American peregrine falcon, the southern sea otter, the gray wolf, and the Aleutian Canada goose. None of these is listed as endangered or is even greatly threatened throughout most of their ranges. However, some species are listed as endangered in part of their ranges, threatened in other parts, and plentiful in still other locations. Therefore, the FWS's efforts have some credibility.

We seem to be somewhat selective about which species we help in their struggle to survive. Some animals are so cute that they are irresistible and receive great press. The giant panda, the Galapagos tortoise, and the elephant seal, for example, have no shortage of champions. Whales intrigue us and gain our support. In the winter of 1989, when three whales were trapped by the ice of the Bering Sea, world attention was drawn to their plight. There was no shortage of interest or funds to see the behemoths to safety. We become alarmed at the drama being played out by tuna fishermen as they inadvertently trap and kill dolphins in their pursuit of food fish. We do not always select the most threatened species to support, instead choosing ones that are cute, endearing, or obviously beneficial to humankind. The Cuban flower bat and the giant anteater, for example, do not evoke great sympathy or attention, even though they are gravely threatened and are indispensable to their environments. These decisions are neither easy nor obvious, relating as they do to the basic ethical questions of animal protection.

SUCCESS STORIES AND THE FUTURE

Not all conservation stories have happy endings. Many of our attempts to save species in this century have not succeeded. The passenger pigeon, for example, was possibly the most numerous of birds in the United States in the 1800s. After being heavily hunted, their numbers became so decimated that the last of the species were captured and kept in zoos. The last passenger pigeon died in the Cincinnati Zoo in 1917. The last dusky beach sparrow died in captivity in 1987. The plight of these creatures was recognized too late to prevent their extinction.

Although humans have been responsible for the elimination of many species, they have also been responsible for helping many species return from the brink of extinction. Many animals have come close to extinction but seem to be making recoveries. Among them are the black-footed ferret, the bison, the bald eagle, the giant panda, the Galapagos tortoise, and the elephant seal.

The Black-Footed Ferret

For several years, the black-footed ferret was thought to be extinct, until a small population was discovered and captured at Meeteetse, Wyoming. These animals had been plentiful on the plains of Wyoming, Nebraska, and Colorado in the 1800s. In March 1987 there were eighteen known black-footed ferrets; today there are over one hundred. The last of the species were captured in Meeteetse and enrolled in a captive breeding program. All of the matings except one were natural. Artificial insemination was used with one pair to reduce inbreeding. Some of the off-spring have been moved from the primary research facility to reduce the risk of *epizootics*, diseases that attack an entire population at once. Ferrets are quite susceptible to being thus overwhelmed. The idea in the ferret breeding program is to establish three to five separate breeding sites with 200 to 250 adult animals at each site. The long-term goal is to reintroduce the animals to the wild as soon as possible. The hope is that 1,500 ferrets will be released in ten different sites in populations of at least 50 per site.

It has been established that black-footed ferrets breed well in captivity. It is not known, however, whether the captive ferrets will be able to resume their natural habits in the wild, that is, whether they still have the hunting skills to prey on prairie dogs. To help in this transition, prairie dog populations are being introduced at the breeding sites so the ferrets can practice hunting before being returned to the wild. The first two captive ferrets were released August 31, 1991, in the Shirley Basin, north of Medicine Bow, Wyoming. Fifty ferrets were released in the same area during September and October of 1991.[3] The ferrets were released on schedule. Apparently they are not doing as well as hoped. They are falling prey to predators, particularly coyotes. Estimates place the survival rate at less than 25 percent.

The American Bison

It is not hard to conjure up the vision of millions of buffalo (bison) roaming the great plains of the western United States and Canada. We have seen the sight in documentaries and in movies depicting the Old West. Bison herds roamed the West in numbers so large that there seemed to be an almost inexhaustible supply of the great beasts.

Native Americans hunted bison for centuries. They killed not wantonly, but out of necessity, for food, ornaments, and clothing. The species was not seriously threatened by this limited intrusion. However, when the westward expansion of non-native settlers began, and particularly when the railroads began cutting through the plains, the outlook for the bison began to shift ominously. First the great beasts were killed for food for the hordes of people working on the railroads. This killing was glorified by sensational stories of the great scout, Buffalo Bill. Next came killing for "sport," as hunting parties shot bison from moving trains, with no thought of using the carcasses. Native Americans were appalled at this practice, which caused more than a little tension between them and the intruders. In a short time, the bison began to disappear. The 50 million bison that were on the plains in the 1800s dwindled to a few hundred individual animals by the 1900s. A rigorous protection program has helped this species increase its population to some 20,000. Their number has increased to the extent that controlled hunting of the bison near Yellowstone National Park was allowed between 1985 and 1990. In this case humans have helped undo the thoughtless deeds of their ancestors.

Will There Be Other Success Stories?

Successful conservation and protection efforts inspire and perhaps encourage further efforts. Still, we will not be able to undo the damage of past human impact—whether from ignorance, malice, or indirect pressure—on *all* threatened species. Difficult decisions about animal protection confront the entire global community, now more than ever as human population increases, encroachment into animals' habitats grows, and the effects of industrial and agricultural pollution spread throughout the world.

The effect of tradition and folklore cannot be ignored, either. For example, the number of black rhinoceroses has fallen from 60,000 in 1970 to 3,500 in 1990,[4] and humans are directly responsible for this 95-percent drop in population. Rhinos have no real enemies in the wild. Humans, however, present a different problem. For centuries many Asians have credited the horn of the rhino with the ability to cure everything from heart disease to heartbreak. Arabs prize the horn for the making of knives. Horns are so much in demand that a single horn brings about $25,000 on the black market. The only solution to this problem is probably to ban dealing in rhino horns. Will such an agreement be made, given the popularity of the horns? Will the black rhino survive?

In this book, we look at ten endangered animal species and see what is being done on their behalf. We examine some apparent successes, report on some failures, and suggest ways in which parents, teachers, and students can become involved in efforts to aid threatened animals. Although many plants are also in danger of becoming extinct, we limit our discussion to the animal kingdom. If this text and the activities in it stimulate the readers to think about the ethical, economic, and practical problems involved in protection of endangered species, our goals for this book will have been achieved.

NOTES

1.   William F. Allman and Joannie M. Schrof, "Can They Be Saved?" *U.S. News and World Report* 107 (October 2, 1989): 52-58.

2.   James Balog, "A Personal Vision of Vanishing Wildlife," *National Geographic* 177 (April 1990): 84-103.

3.   Patrick O'Driscoll, "Wyoming Celebrates Return of the Ferrets," *The Denver Post* (September 1, 1991): C-1 to C-2.

4.   Jessica Speart, "Animal House: Suspended in Icy Liquid Nitrogen, Snow Leopards, Tigers, and Rhino Wait for Life at the Cincinnati Zoo," *Omni* 12 (August 1990): 22.

RESOURCE BIBLIOGRAPHY

Books

Burt, Olive W. *Rescued! America's Endangered Wildlife on the Comeback Trail*. New York: Julian Messner, 1980.
    The author details several projects that are helping endangered animals. She tells of rescue efforts to save the alligator, the peregrine falcon, the whooping crane, and others.

Crowe, Philip Kingsland. *The Empty Ark: Travels in Search of Vanishing Wildlife*. New York: Charles Scribner's Sons, 1967.
    This book is an account of three journeys the author made on behalf of the World Wildlife Fund, during which he met with the leaders of several countries to ask what was being done to aid threatened and endangered species.

Facklam, Margery. *And Then There Was One: The Mysteries of Extinction*. San Francisco: Sierra Club Books; Boston: Little, Brown, 1990.
    The author looks at reasons for extinction and near extinction of animals and tells some success stories about helping animals near extinction start on the road to recovery. Legislation and special programs that have helped pressured animals are discussed. Illustrations are by Pamela Johnson.

Lear, Edward. *The Scroobious Pip*. Completed by Ogden Nash. Illustrated by Nancy Ekholm Burkert. New York: Harper & Row Junior Books, 1968.
    Lear's delightful poem about the inscrutable Scroobious Pip has been completed by Ogden Nash and lushly illustrated by Nancy Ekholm Burkert. The verses celebrate the infinite variety in nature and implicitly demand that we do our best to preserve that variety.

Murray, John A. *Wildlife in Peril: The Endangered Mammals of Colorado*. Boulder, Colo.: Rinehart, 1987.
   Discusses the endangerment of several species indigenous to Colorado including the river otter, black-footed ferret, wolverine, lynx, grizzly bear, and the gray wolf.

Olsen, Jack. *Slaughter the Animals, Poison the Earth*. New York: Simon and Schuster, 1971.
   This book looks at the plight of the misunderstood predators of the American West, including wildcats, wolves, eagles, bears, mountain lions, and coyotes, and the factors pushing them all toward extinction.

Roever, J. M. *The Black-Footed Ferret*. Austin, Tex.: Steck-Vaughn Company, 1972.
   The natural history of this member of the weasel family is discussed in this book for young readers.

Magazine Articles

Allman, William F., and Joannie M. Schrof. "Can They Be Saved?" *U.S. News and World Report* 107 (October 2, 1989): 52-58.
   This article traces the economic realities of endangered species, particularly the African elephant. An interesting graph of the location of endangered animals shows winners and losers in the struggle.

Balog, James. "A Personal Vision of Vanishing Wildlife." *National Geographic* 177 (April 1990): 84-103.
   An excellent photographic essay of some of the endangered animals of the world that uses a technique most often found in commercial advertising photography. The result is a stunning portfolio of several endangered animals in poses and settings in which they have never before been seen.

Budiansky, Stephen. "More Environmental Than Thou." *U.S. News and World Report* 108 (March 26, 1990): 10-11.
   This article traces the comeback of the bald eagle and cites humankind as both destroyer and savior of the species.

"Endangered Species Need More Help." *Science News* 135 (February 1989): 79.
   This news column tells of the plans and shortcomings of federal agencies in helping endangered species.

O'Driscoll, Patrick. "Wyoming Celebrates Return of the Ferrets." *The Denver Post* (September 1, 1991): C-1 to C-2.

Reiger, George. "Why Save Endangered Species?" *Field and Stream* 93 (January 1989): 15, 17.
   This article gives a sportsperson's point of view toward saving endangered species and cites reasons why even little-known species should be helped in their fight for survival.

Speart, Jessica. "Animal House: Suspended in Icy Liquid Nitrogen, Snow Leopards, Tigers, and Rhino Wait for Life at the Cincinnati Zoo." *Omni* 12 (August 1990): 22.
   The author tells of the efforts of Betsy Dresser, a reproductive physiologist, to preserve eggs, sperm, and developing embryos of endangered species cryonically by placing them in straws submerged in liquid nitrogen. The materials will be used in the future to help regenerate rare species.

THE WOLF AND THE SEVEN LITTLE KIDS

Collected by Jacob and Wilhelm Grimm

nce upon a time, there was an old nanny goat who had seven little kids. She loved them with all the love of a mother for her children. One day she wanted to go into the forest and fetch some food, so she called all seven kids to her and said, "Dear children, I must leave you to go into the forest. Be on your guard against the wolf, for if he comes in, he will devour you—skin, hair, and all. The wretch often disguises himself, but you will know him at once by his rough voice and his black feet."

The kids said, "Dear mother, we will take good care of ourselves; you may go away without any anxiety." The old one bleated and went on her way with an easy mind.

It was not long before someone knocked at the door and cried, "Open the door, dear children; your mother is here and has brought something back with her for each of you."

But the little kids knew that it was the wolf, by his rough voice. "We will not open the door," cried they, "you are not our mother. She has a soft, pleasant voice, but your voice is rough; you are the wolf!" The wolf went away to a shopkeeper and bought himself a great lump of chalk. He ate the chalk and made his voice soft with it.

Then he came back, knocked at the door of the house, and cried, "Open the door, dear children, your mother is here and has brought something back with her for each of you."

But the wolf had laid his black paws against the window, and the children saw them and cried, "We will not open the door. Our mother does not have black feet like you: you are the wolf!"

Then the wolf ran to a baker and said, "I have hurt my feet; rub some dough over them for me." And when the baker had rubbed the wolf's feet, the wolf ran to the miller and said, "Rub some white flour over my feet for

9

me." The miller thought to himself, "The wolf wants to deceive someone," and refused, but the wolf said, "If you will not do it, I will devour you." Then the miller was afraid, so he made the wolf's paws white for him.

Now the wretch went for the third time to the house door, knocked at it, and said, "Open the door for me, children! Your dear little mother has come home, and has brought every one of you something back from the forest with her."

The little kids cried, "First show us your paws that we may know if you are our dear little mother." Then the wolf put his paws up to the window, and when the kids saw that they were white, they believed that all he said was true and opened the door. But who should come in but the wolf!

The kids were terrified and tried to hide themselves. One sprang under the table, the second into the bed, the third into the stove, the fourth into the kitchen, the fifth into the cupboard, the sixth under the washing bowl, and the seventh into the clock case. But the wolf found them, and used no great ceremony; one after the other, he swallowed them down his throat. The youngest, who had hidden in the clock case, was the only one he did not find. When the wolf had satisfied his appetite he took himself off, lay down under a tree in the green meadow outside, and went to sleep.

Soon afterwards the old mother goat came home again from the forest. What a sight she saw there! The door of the house stood wide open. The table, chairs, and benches were thrown down, the washing bowl lay broken to pieces, and the quilts and pillows were pulled off the bed. She sought her children, but they were nowhere to be found. She called them one after another by name, but no one answered. At last, when she came to the youngest, a soft voice cried, "Dear mother, I am in the clock case." She took the kid out and it told her that the wolf had come and eaten all the others. Then you may imagine how she wept over her poor children.

At length in her grief she went out and the youngest kid ran with her. When they came to the meadow, there lay the wolf by the tree, snoring so loudly that the branches shook. The mother goat looked at the wolf on every side and saw that something was moving and struggling in his gorged body. "Ah, heavens," said she, "is is possible that my poor children, whom he has swallowed down for his supper, can be still alive?"

Then the kid ran home and fetched scissors and a needle and thread. The mother goat began to cut open the monster's stomach. Hardly had she made one cut than one little kid thrust its head out. When she cut farther, all six sprang out one after another. They were all still alive and had suffered no injury whatever, for in his greediness the wolf had swallowed them down whole. What rejoicing there was! They all embraced their dear mother and jumped for joy all around the meadow.

The mother, however, said, "Now go and look for some big stones, and we will fill the wicked beast's stomach with them while he is still asleep." Then the seven kids dragged large stones to their mother with all speed, and put as many of them into the wolf's stomach as they could get in. The mother sewed him up again in the greatest haste, so that he was not aware of anything and never once stirred.

When the wolf at length had had enough sleep, he got to his feet and decided to go to a well to drink, as the stones in his stomach made him very thirsty. But when he tried to walk and to move about, the stones in his stomach knocked against each other and rattled. Then cried he,

> What rumbles and tumbles
> against my poor bones?
> I thought 'twas six kids,
> But it's naught but big stones.

When the wolf got to the well, he stooped over the water and was just about to drink when the heavy stones shifted and made him fall in. There was no help and the old wolf drowned miserably. When the seven kids saw that, they came running to the spot and cried aloud, "The wolf is dead! The wolf is dead!" and danced for joy round about the well with their mother.

▶●◀

FOLKLORE

Wolves have been stereotyped in western European folklore and language for thousands of years. Figures of speech, such as "wolf in sheep's clothing," "wolf whistle," "cry wolf," "wolf pack," "wolf your food down," "lone wolf," and "she wolf," demonstrate the value judgments humans have placed on wolves. They are all negative reactions. Many of these wolf references can be found in collections of Aesop's fables.

The Bible uses the wolf as a symbol of evil. "Beware of false prophets, who come to you in the clothing of sheep, but inwardly they are ravening wolves ... (Matthew 7:15). Behold, I send you as sheep in the midst of wolves ... (Matthew 10:16). I know that after my departure, ravening wolves will enter among you, not sparing the flock (Acts 20:29). According to the Bible, wolves are vicious, false, and evil. The kindest thing the Bible has to say for the wolf is in Isaiah 11:6, "The wolf and the lamb will lie down together and the leopards and goats will be at peace. Calves and fat cattle will be safe among lions, and a little child shall lead them all." As far as kindness goes, the wolves are categorized with leopards and lions—all of them obviously dangerous.

In pre-Christian Europe, however, the wolf was a popular clan totem. People who claimed the wolf as an ancestor believed that, with the invocation of specific sacred rites and rituals, they could become wolves or be turned into wolves. In ancient Egypt, the wolf god Up-Uat, who predated Horus and Anubis, was called "Opener of the Way" or "Opener of the Body." The Great Goddess, as "the great she-wolf," was the focus of the early Roman cult of Lupa. She was the "Mother of the Wolves," the divine midwife, the mother of the ancestral spirits, and foster mother to Romulus and Remus, the twins who founded the city of Rome. Numerous folklores include similar tales of a nurse wolf who nurtures human children.

The wolf is a symbol of winter, darkness, and an omen of death. The Germanic gods donned wolfskins to signify the solar hero hidden by the night or the dark of winter and removed the wolfskins to signify the light of day and spring. The wolf of evening succeeds in his wickedness, swallowing the hero and taking him into the underworld. The wolf of evening is foiled by the brilliance of the rising hero of the dawn. The morning wolf and the springtime wolf triumph until vanquished by the evening and winter wolves, thus describing the ancient cycles.

This duality may explain the diverse characteristics ascribed to the wolf in common lore. On the one hand, the good wolf defends the faith and the faithful and has curative powers. For example, wolf teeth rubbed over the gums of teething children were believed to relieve pain; wearing a wolf's head brought courage; wearing a wolfskin made children strong and brave; and a wolf bite rendered one invulnerable and impervious to pain. On the other hand, the diabolical and perfidious wolf was the master of wickedness and perversity. He was the thief on the road; an evil, malignant spirit; a fradulent, double-dealing, deceiving, beast capable of witchcraft and murderous intent.

Other folk beliefs concerning wolves include the following:

- To sleep well, put a wolf's head under the pillow.

- A wolfskin coat guards its wearer against hydrophobia (rabies).

- Sprinkle salt in a wolf's tracks to keep the wolf away.

- Wolf's milk purifies the skin.

- To be seen by a wolf before you see the wolf means that you will lose your powers of speech.

- To make a wolf drop a stolen livestock animal, drop an object from your pocket.

- Saying the name of the wolf even once during the Twelve Days of Christmas invites the wolf to your door.

In European folktales, the werewolf is usually a person by day and a wolf by night, possibly the victim of a wicked enchantment. At daybreak, he hides his wolfskin. Some stories tell that it is possible to break such a spell by pointing at the werewolf while he is in his human form and shouting, "You are the wolf!" However, the enchantment may be transferred to the accusing person.

Native American folk beliefs have a more positive image of the wolf. The Wolf Clan is one of the eight clans of the Seneca. For some tribes, the Wolf Spirit is a teacher who offers many lessons for those willing to look beyond physical boundaries. The Wolf Spirit is responsible for singing the moon into the sky. Native Americans respect the wolf because it is family-oriented and social by nature. Wolves are also cooperative hunters, skilled at survival, and are good providers for their families.

The following story, from George Bird Grinnell's *By Cheyenne Campfires*,[1] is an example of the wolf as helper and mystical protector. It certainly portrays the wolf in a more positive light than the one in most European folklore, although it parallels some of the aspects of traditional nurse-wolf lore.

The Wolf Helper*

After the Sand Creek massacre was over, and the troops had gone, there were left alive two women. In 1902 these women were still living. One was named Two She-Wolf Woman, and the other, Standing in Different Places Woman. They were sisters, and each had a little daughter—one ten years old and one of six years. Their husband was badly wounded and likely to die, and he told them they must leave him and go on home to the camp, so that they might save themselves and their children. They started. They had no food, and no implements except their knives and a little short-handled axe. They had their robes.

They traveled on and on, until they reached the Smoky Hill River. Here they found many rose berries, and they pounded them up with the little axe and ate them. After they had pounded the rose berries they made flat cakes of them to give to the children, and started on. They did not know where the camp was, and did not know where to go. They just followed the river down.

One night after they had been traveling for six or seven days, they went into a little hole in the bluff for shelter, for it was very cold. They were sitting up, one robe under them, with the other in front of them, and with the children lying between them. In the middle of the night something came into the hole and lay down by them, and when this thing had come near to them, standing between them and the opening of the hole, they saw that it was a big wolf, and were afraid of it; but it lay down quietly.

Next morning they started on, and the wolf went with them, walking not far to one side of them. Their feet were sore, for their moccasins were worn out, and they often stopped to rest, and when they did so the wolf lay down near by. At one of these halts the elder woman spoke to the wolf, just as she would talk to a person. She said to him: "O Wolf, try to do something for us. We and our children are nearly starved." When she spoke to him, the wolf seemed to listen and rose up on his haunches and looked at her, and when she stopped speaking he rose to his feet and started off toward the north. It was the early part of the winter, but there was no snow on the ground.

The women still sat there resting, for they were weak and tired and footsore. They saw the wolf pass out of sight over the hill, and after a time they saw him coming back. He came toward them, and when he was close to them they could see that his mouth and jaws were covered with blood. He stepped in front of them and turned his head and looked back in the

*Story taken from *By Cheyenne Campfires* by George Bird Grinnell, copyright © 1926, 1962 (New Haven, Conn.: Yale University Press).

direction from whence he had come. The women were so weak and stiff they could hardly get up, but they rose to their feet. When they stood up the wolf trotted off to the top of the hill and stopped, looking back, and they followed him very slowly. When they reached the top of the hill and looked off, they saw, down in the little draw beyond, the carcass of a buffalo, and in a circle all about it sat many wolves. The wolf looked back at the women again, and then loped down toward the carcass. Now the women started to walk fast toward the carcass, for here was food. All the wolves still sat about; they were not feeding on the carcass.

When the women reached it they drew their knives and opened it. They made no fire, but at once ate the liver and tripe, and the fat about the intestines, without cooking, and gave food to the children. Then they cut off pieces of the meat, as much as they could carry, and made up packs and started on their way. As soon as they had left the carcass, all the wolves fell upon it and began to eat it quickly, growling and snarling at each other, and soon they had eaten it all. The big wolf ate with the other wolves. The women went on over the hill and stopped; they had eaten so much that they could not go far. In the evening, when the sun was low, one of the women said to the other, "Here is our friend again"; and the wolf came trotting up to them.

Soon after he had joined them they started on to look for a hollow where they might sleep. The wolf traveled with them. When it grew dark they stopped, and the wolf lay near them. Every day they tried to find a place to camp where there were willows. They used to cut these and make a shelter of them, and cover this with grass, and make a bed of grass, and then put down their robes and cover themselves with grass. So they were well sheltered.

One morning as they were going along they looked over the hill and saw in the bottom below them some ponies feeding. They started down to see whose they were, the wolf traveling along, but off to one side. Before they had come near to the horses two persons came up over a hill, and when these persons saw the women coming they sprang on their horses and ran away fast. The women walked on to the place where the men had been. Here there was a fire, and meat that the men had left—a tongue and other food roasting. The women took the meat and ate, and they cut the tongue in two and gave the smaller end of it to the wolf, which had come up and was lying by the fire.

After they had finished eating they went on, and soon came to a big spring with a hollow near by—a good place to camp. They were glad to find the place, for the sky looked as if it were going to snow. They made a good camp, a house of willows and grass, and covered it with bark from the trees. By this time they had become so accustomed to having the wolf with them that every night they used to make a bed near the door of the house, piling up grass for him to sleep on.

That night the women heard a noise down in the hollow—something calling like a big owl. Two She-Wolf Woman was watching; for they were afraid during the night, and used to take turns keeping watch. They could hear this thing breaking sticks as it walked about. The watcher awoke her sister, saying, "Wake up! something is coming." The wolf now stood up, and soon he began to howl with a long-drawn-out cry, which was very dismal. Soon from all directions many wolves began to come to the place. After a little while this thing that was making the noise began to come closer, and when it did so all the wolves rushed toward it and began fighting it, and the women seized their children and ran away into the night. They got far out on the level prairie and stopped there, for their feet were sore, and they were very tired. In the morning just as day was breaking they saw the big wolf coming toward them. When he reached them he lay down.

The elder woman now spoke to him again, and said, "Wolf, take pity on us; help us to find the trail of our people." When she had ceased speaking, the wolf trotted away, leaving the women, and they followed on very slowly. Before long they saw him coming back toward them fast—loping. When he got to them they saw that he had in his mouth a big piece of dried meat. He dropped the meat in front of them. They seized the meat and divided it, and gave some of it to their children and ate of it themselves. The wolf did not lie down, but stood waiting, and when they had eaten, he led them to an old camp where there were sticks standing in the ground, and on each stick hung a parfleche sack of meat. Their relations had left these things for them, knowing that they were lost and thinking that they might pass that way.

Now the women had plenty of food; they went to the water and built a shelter with a place in it for the wolf. That night it snowed. When they arose the snow was above their ankles. Again the woman spoke to the wolf, and asked him to go and find their camp, and he went away. The women stayed there. The wolf was not gone a long time; he came back the same day. They were watching for him, for now they knew that he was their friend, and that he was true; they knew that he would do something for them. The two women went to the top of the little hill near by, and before night they saw the wolf coming. He came up to them and stopped, and then began to look back. The women felt sure that he had found something, and went back to their camp and got their children, and went to the wolf, who started back as he had come, traveling ahead of them. On the point of a high hill he stopped, and when the women overtook him they looked down, and there they saw a big Cheyenne camp on the river below. This was the head of the Republican River.

They went on down to the camp, and to the lodge of Gray Beard. The wolf remained on the hill. After the women had eaten, the older woman took meat, and told the people that a wolf had led them to the camp, and she was going back to give him something to eat. She went back and gave the wolf the food, and after he had eaten she said to him, "Now, you have brought us to the camp, you can go back to your old ways." Late that evening the woman went up on the hill again to see if the wolf was there, but he was gone. She saw his tracks going back the same way that he had come. This happened in the winter of 1864 and 1865. The women and one of the children are still alive.

► ● ◄

The words of Chief Dan George, hereditary chief for the Salish tribe and honorary chief for the Squamish tribe in the Pacific Northwest, explain people's conflicting attitudes toward wolves best:

> If you talk to the animals
>   they will talk with you
>   and you will know each other.
> If you do not talk to them
>   you will not know them,
> And what you do not know
>   you will fear.
> What one fears
>   one destroys.

DISCUSSION

Description

The wolf is a wild animal resembling a large German Shepherd dog. Its legs are longer than those of the German Shepherd and its feet larger. Other differences include: its jaws are stronger, its head is wider, its ears always stand up straight, and it always has a long, bushy tail. Male wolves usually weigh more than 100 pounds (45.4 kilograms) and they can travel for hours at about 20 miles (32 kilometers) per hour.

Wolves may be white, gray, brown, or black. Generally, wolves of the northern and arctic regions are lighter in color than those of the southern forests. The arctic wolf, which may be pure white, has often been bred with domestic dogs to produce a strong, hardy sled dog. Two species of wolf are native to North America: the gray wolf (or timber wolf) and the red wolf. Scientists have identified thirty-two subspecies of the gray wolf in North America.

Behavior

Wolves have strong family ties and they often mate for life. Two months after mating usually in April or May, the female has from four to six pups in a den dug in the earth. The pups are blind for about a week after birth. Both wolf parents feed and train the pups. They remain in family groups for quite a while; in fact, wolf packs are simply family groups. They communicate with each other through their howls. Jim Bridger, American pioneer and scout in the late 1880s, noted that wolves signaled to each other and understood each other the same as men.

Pups spend their days chasing grasshoppers, field mice, and gophers. Although they also eat smaller mammals and rodents, wolves in the wild usually prey on caribou, moose, and deer, selecting weaker animals as their meal. In reality, wolves form a vital part of the natural community. Because they kill sick or injured animals, they keep caribou, moose, and deer herds in a healthy condition. As humans move into their territory, bringing with them domestic animals, cattle and sheep have been added to the wolves' diet.

Habitat

Wolves prefer to live in forested areas with trees and thick brush. The name *timber wolf* is indicative of their presence in heavily wooded regions.

Historic Range

Wolves live in North America, Greenland, Europe, and Asia. The howl of the wolf was once heard in almost every part of North America from Alaska to Mexico and from the Atlantic to the Pacific oceans. Great Plains wolves used to follow the buffalo herds on the Great Plains of North America. When the buffalo were destroyed, the wolves turned to cattle and sheep for food. The ranchers hunted and poisoned them to extinction. Today wolves may be found in northern Canada, Alaska, and a few wilderness areas in the contiguous United States.

Reasons for Endangerment and Attempts to Help

Civilization has invaded the wolf's habitat until today they are in danger of extinction. Some wolf species, such as the gray and red, still survive in the wild, while others, such as the Great Plains or buffalo, have become extinct. Farmers and ranchers used to kill many wolves to protect their livestock. In fact, the government offered bounties (rewards) for wolf pelts (skins), which were proof of kill. In 1943 a government trapper shot the last free-roaming timber wolf in Colorado. Today there are efforts to reintroduce the wolf into wilderness areas. These animals, once shot on sight, are now being aided by their former enemies.

A newspaper report from Missoula, Montana, tells of an amazing response from people offering to help six orphaned wolf pups. The animals are protected by the Endangered Species Act and are part of a federal program to establish ten breeding pairs of wolves in Montana. The pups' mother was illegally shot to death and the father wolf, who then fed and protected the pups, was hit by a car on Interstate 90. Federal officials stepped in and are feeding the pups road-killed animals.

Both the gray and red wolf are making a comeback, but their presence has sparked heated controversy. Debates about reintroducing the wolf to Yellowstone Park are raging today. There seems to be no middle ground—one either hopes that the wolf will once again take its place in the natural scheme of things or one wants to see every last one of them killed. Not only concern for livestock but also folklore beliefs contribute to this irrational hatred of the animal.

WOLF ACTIVITIES

Wolves as Stereotypes

- Brainstorm all the things you think or feel when the word *wolf* is mentioned. If your reaction is mostly negative, reflect and discuss why this might be.

- Bring in pictures of wolves. Are there stereotypes? How is the stereotyping of wolves similar to those of other peoples or of different countries and cultures?

- What other animals are stereotyped? (For example, pigs and turkeys.) Why have they been stereotyped? Write a story stereotyping another animal.

- Brainstorm positive aspects of wolves. Research the literature for additional positive aspects of wolves.

- Create posters or bumper stickers with slogans that encourage positive feelings toward wolves.

- Brainstorm remedies to the stereotyping of wolves. Get together in small groups and discuss what you can do to eliminate the stereotyping.

Wolves and the Environment

- Discuss how animals adapt to new environments and the possible consequences of not adapting.

- Research wolf tracks. Make a transparency of the tracks. Discuss how wolves hide or escape from their predators.

- Discuss preparations wolves make for winter. Illustrate their preparations on a poster.

- Keep an imaginary journal of the life of a wolf for five days.

- Make a concentration game with cards of pictures of animals on half the cards and their habitats on the other half.

Wolves as an Endangered Species

- Brainstorm the things you think have contributed to wolves' becoming endangered.

- Research the laws in your state concerning killing wolves. How have these laws changed?

- Research why wolfhounds were developed.

- Collect newspaper and magazine articles about the studies or research done on wolves or their reintroduction into former habitats. Use this information for a bulletin board on wolves.

- Relate the similarities and differences of what is happening to the wolf today and what has happened in the past. (Refer to current newspaper and magazine articles and books like *The Last Wolf of Ireland*.)

- Discuss the impact of restrictions on killing wolves. Predict what you think the future for wolves will be.

- Write an article or advertisement describing the wolf and convince your audience of the importance of their existence.

- Make a poster that charts what you have learned in your research.

Wolves and the Arts

- Sculpt a wolf from clay. Make a mural of wolves in the wild as a backdrop for the sculptures.

- Make wolf puppets. Produce a puppet play advertising the wolf that convinces the audience of the importance of the wolf's survival. Write a song about wolves to include in the play.

- Build a wolf mask and use it in a play or song presentation (see fig. 2.1, pages 20-22 for directions).

Wolves in Literature

- Investigate the legend of the werewolf. Where did it come from? Is it still believed?

- Assemble a stack of children's books and comics about or including wolves. Look through and divide them into "wolves that are real" and "wolves that are unreal." Share examples of both. Name three things an imaginary animal does that a real animal cannot do. Discuss what makes animals real and what makes them unreal.
  1. Discuss the importance of being able to tell when something is real and when something is make-believe. Discuss why this distinction is important to remember when learning about animals and how they live.
  2. Compare examples of animals as portrayed in these books and comics for a variety of categories: sounds they make, shelter, appearance, actions, food, movement, etc. Chart these examples.

- Several picture books of *Peter and the Wolf* are listed in the bibliography. Compare and contrast these different books with the musical piece by Sergei Prokofiev. How are they alike? How are they different? Play the music and discuss which instrument represents what character in the story. Describe what the instruments sound like. Discuss other ways to portray animals with other musical instruments. Act out the story.

- Read several folkstories with wolves as the main characters. Discuss where the stories take place, exploring the geography and environment.

- There are a variety of books in the bibliography based on the story of *Little Red Riding Hood*. Compare and contrast these versions. Repeat this for *The Three Little Pigs*, including Jon Scieszka's *The True Story of the Three Little Pigs*, which is told from the wolf's point of view. Rewrite a folktale from the point of view of the wolf. Variations of this activity could include newspaper articles, society-page articles, letters to Ann Wolfers, a mock trial for the wolf, and so forth. Another variation is to rewrite while concentrating on using synonyms. For example, "Little Red Riding Hood initiated plans for the preparation, transportation, and delivery of nutritious gifts to a senior citizen relative."

(Text continues on page 23.)

Directions for Making a Wolf Mask

The mask as shown in this figure measures only about 6 inches by 8.5 inches. The actual size of the mask should be about 11 inches by 17 inches. You can enlarge these pages in one of two ways. First, you can copy the page from the book and take it to a commercial print shop and have it enlarged to 11 inches by 17 inches (folio size). Another way is to use an opaque projector. Project the image on a sheet of tagboard or construction material, adjust the size of the image until it is 11 inches by 17 inches, and then trace the image. There are two sides to the mask design printed here as front and back. Once you have your mask pattern, follow these directions:

1. Cut out the mask along the dotted lines.

2. Fold the muzzle piece along the thick solid line between the ears.

3. Use crayons or markers to color in wolf markings.

4. Pull the ear tabs forward and glue at the "x"s.

5. Place glue on the side pieces, then attach to the back of the mask at the "x"s.

6. Attach an elastic chin strap to the holes on the side pieces. The mask may be worn on top of the head or pulled down so you can look out the eye holes.

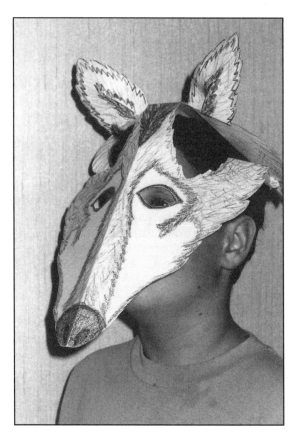

Fig. 2.1. The wolf mask (directions and patterns). (Photograph courtesy of Deborah McGlathery.)

Fig. 2.1. — *Continued*

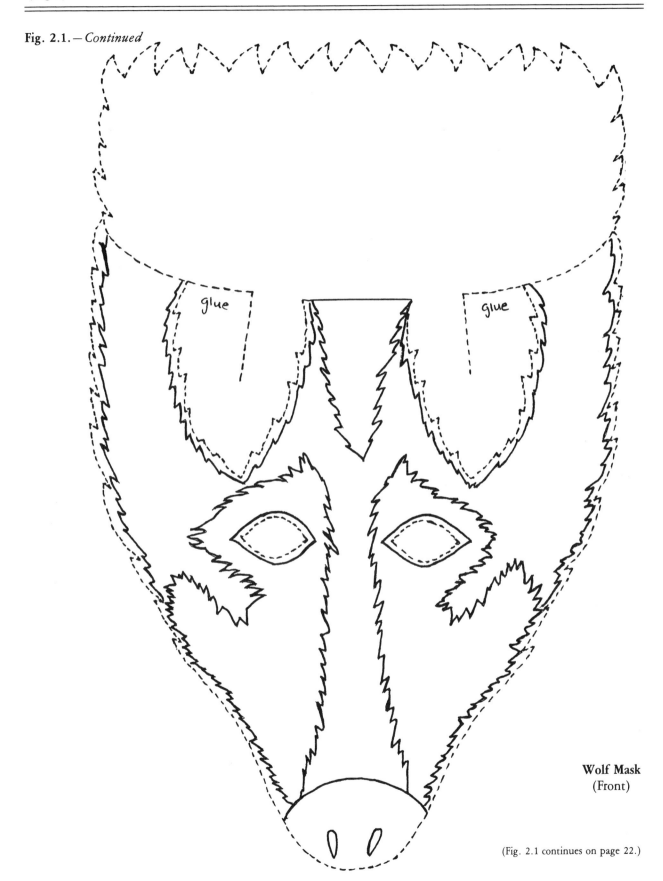

glue

glue

Wolf Mask
(Front)

(Fig. 2.1 continues on page 22.)

Fig. 2.1. — *Continued*

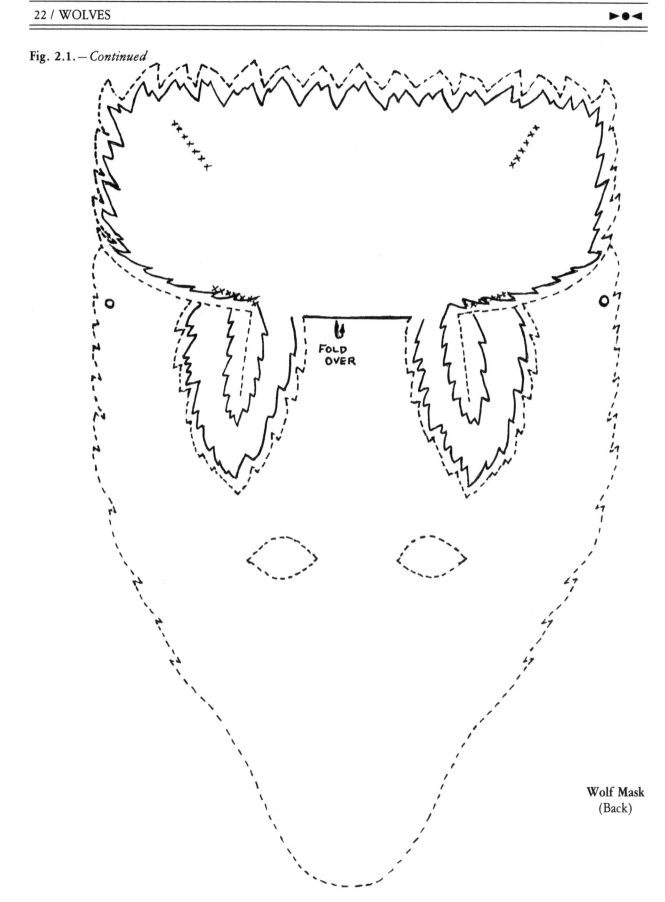

FOLD
OVER

Wolf Mask
(Back)

• Adapt a folktale with a wolf as one of the main characters into a readers' theatre script. Use the following script as an example, but create your own script.

The Dog and the Wolf

Cast of characters:

    Narrator
    House Dog (a pet)
    Wolf

Narrator: Aesop, a slave in the sixth century B.C., collected and told many fables. It was said that he won his freedom by his storytelling talents. "The Dog and the Wolf" is adapted from Aesop's fable of the same name. The fable begins when a wolf, half dead with hunger, comes upon a house dog.

House Dog: (energetically) Hey, brother wolf, what's happening?

Wolf: (in a very sad voice) Nothing, lately. In fact, I haven't had anything to eat for days.

House Dog: I can see that! Look at you, you can hardly stand up. You must be weak from hunger.

Wolf: (very weakly) I know, but what can I do? I can never know when I'll get my next meal.

House Dog: Now that's a problem. (Pause) Maybe I have a deal for you. Come with me to my master and share my work. The work is hard, but the food is regular and good.

Narrator: And so they went, the jovial, well-fed house dog gaily leading the frail, weak wolf.
    (Pause)
As they were making their way towards the town, the wolf noticed something peculiar about the house dog. He questioned him.

Wolf: Hey, dog, how did the hair on your neck get worn away?

House Dog: Oh, this? (Pointing to one side of his neck) That's nothing. That's where my master puts the collar on me at night when he chains me up. Yes, it rubs a bit, but I do get fed each day. You don't get something for nothing.

Narrator: When he heard this, the wolf suddenly stopped, turned around, and started slowly walking back to where they came from.

House Dog: (impatiently) Hey! Where are you going? You can't leave now. We are going to work together.

Wolf: No way! Good-bye, house dog. To me it's better to starve free than to be a fat slave.

Narrator: With that, the wolf went on his way to enjoy his free — if sometimes hungry — life.

NOTES

1. George Bird Grinnell, *By Cheyenne Campfires* (Lincoln: University of Nebraska Press, 1971), 149-53.

RESOURCE BIBLIOGRAPHY

Books

Bradman, Tony, and Margaret Chamberlain. *Who's Afraid of the Big Bad Wolf?* New York: Macmillan/Aladdin, 1989.
This is a lift-the-flap version of the familiar tale in which three little pigs deal with the big bad wolf.

Delaney, A. *The Gunnywolf*. New York: Harper & Row, 1988.
A little girl wanders into the woods to pick flowers and meets the dreaded Gunnywolf.

Dettmer, Mary Lou. *Little Red Riding Hood*. Morton Grove, Ill.: Whitman, 1971.
In this version, the wolf runs away, chased by the woodsman.

Gay, Michel. *The Christmas Wolf*. New York: Greenwillow, 1980.
When his children wonder why Father Christmas does not come to their mountain, Father Wolf goes to town to shop for Christmas presents, with unforeseen results.

George, Jean Craighead. *Julie of the Wolves*. New York: Harper & Row, 1972.
While running away from home and an unwanted marriage, a thirteen-year-old Eskimo girl becomes lost on the North Slope of Alaska and is befriended by a wolf pack.

_____. *The Moon of the Gray Wolves*. Illustrated by Sal Catalano. New York: HarperCollins, 1991.
Describes the experience of a wolf pack in Toklat Pass in Alaska during the November moon.

_____. *The Wounded Wolf*. Illustrated by John Schoenherr. New York: Harper & Row, 1978.
Hungry animals close in on an injured wolf, hoping to feed on him, when help arrives. Told through poetic text.

Goble, Paul. *Dream Wolf*. New York: Bradbury, 1990.
Native Americans have wonderful stories about wolves who helped women and children when they were lost or in danger. There are also stories of wounded men, far from home and help, whom the wolves fed until they recovered. This is the story of two lost Plains Indian children who are cared for and guided safely home by a friendly wolf.

Grimm, Jacob, and Wilhelm Grimm. *Grimm's Complete Fairy Tales*. New York: Nelson Doubleday, n.d.
There are several stories with wolf characters in this collection: "The Wolf and the Seven Little Kids," "The Wolf and the Fox," "The Wolf and the Man," "Gossip Wolf and the Fox," and "Little Red Riding Hood."

_____. *Little Red Riding Hood*. Illustrated by Bernadette. New York: Scholastic, 1971.
The art as well as the story variation make this version of the tale special.

Grinnell, George Bird. *By Cheyenne Campfires*. Lincoln: University of Nebraska Press, 1971.
A collection of stories and experiences from interviews with Native Americans.

Harper, Wilhelmina. *The Gunniwolf*. Illustrated by William Wiesner. New York: Dutton, 1967.
A little girl is out picking flowers and she forgets her grandmother's warning. She has an adventure with the fierce old Gunniwolf.

Hyman, Trina Schart. *Little Red Riding Hood*. New York: Holiday House, 1983.
This is an award-winning, illustrated version of the classic folktale. Can you discover why this version has been challenged by some people?

Ling, Mary. *Eyewitness Juniors: Amazing Wolves, Dogs, and Foxes*. Photographs by Jerry Young. New York: Knopf, 1991.
The gray wolf is introduced in text and photographs.

Livo, Norma J., and Sandra A. Rietz. *Storytelling Folklore Sourcebook*. Englewood, Colo.: Libraries Unlimited, 1990.
This collection of folklore references and information from around the world includes stories of animal tricksters.

Lopez, Barry Holstun. *Of Wolves and Men*. New York: Scribner's, 1978.
Contains a wealth of observation, mythology, and mysticism as well as an absorbing section on biology. An extremely popular account of the wolf.

Malterre, Elona. *The Last Wolf of Ireland*. New York: Clarion, 1990.
Despite the frightening stories they have heard about wolves, a boy and girl, living in Ireland in the 1780s, attempt to defy authority and save the last wolf left in the country.

McPhail, David. *A Wolf Story*. New York: Scribner's, 1981.
Following his escape from a movie set, a timber wolf is hunted by police and soldiers until a group of children arrange for the wolf to be set free.

Morris, Ann. *The Little Red Riding Hood Rebus Book*. Illustrated by Ljiljana Rylands. New York: Orchard Books, 1987.
A rebus version of the fairy tale about the little girl who meets a hungry wolf in the forest, in which pictures are substituted for some words or parts of words.

Mowat, Farley. *Never Cry Wolf*. New York: Franklin Watts, 1963.
A story based on the idea from Aesop's fable.

Patent, Dorothy Hinshaw. *Gray Wolf, Red Wolf*. Photographs by William Munoz. New York: Clarion, 1990.
Describes the physical characteristics, life cycle, and behavior of the two species of wolves found in North America. It also discusses efforts to save them from extinction by reintroducing them to wilderness areas. Another strong point, for reference, is a list of addresses for information on the wolf.

Perrault, Charles. *Little Red Riding Hood*. Illustrated by Sarah Moon. Mankato, Minn.: Creative Education, 1983.
Illustrated with black-and-white pictures of a real little girl, this book won an international graphic art award. It has also been the object of much criticism.

Prokofiev, Sergei. *Peter and the Wolf*. Illustrated by Warren Chappell. New York: Knopf, 1940.
  The story of *Peter and the Wolf* is accompanied by musical instruments that represent the story characters.

———. *Peter and the Wolf*. Retold by Ann King Herring. Tokyo, Japan: Gakken, 1971.
  This version of *Peter and the Wolf* is illustrated by Kozo Shimizu through collages.

———. *Peter and the Wolf*. Retold by Loriot. Illustrated by Jorg Muller. New York: Knopf, 1986.
  This version is published in a book-and-cassette format. The music on the cassette is performed by the Hamburg Symphony Orchestra.

———. *Peter and the Wolf*. Illustrated by Josef Palecek. Saxonville, Mass.: Picture Book Studio, 1987.
  The orchestra version retells the fairy tale of a boy who ignores his grandfather's warnings and goes out to capture a wolf.

Sara. *The Rabbit, the Fox, and the Wolf*. New York: Orchard Books, 1991.
  After a wolf saves a rabbit chased by a fox, the wolf and rabbit become friends.

Scally, Kevin. *The Story of Red Riding Hood*. New York: Grosset & Dunlap, 1984.
  On almost every page, the reader must make a decision about the way the story will develop. By following the directions, the reader can be sent anywhere in the book—not necessarily forward.

Scieszka, Jon. *The True Story of the Three Little Pigs*. Illustrated by Lane Smith. New York: Viking Kestrel, 1989.
  The wolf gives his own outlandish version of what really happened when he tangled with the three little pigs.

Stone, George. *A Legend of Wolf Song*. New York: Grosset & Dunlap, 1975.
  A dramatic and moving story that provides not only an accurate picture of the life of the wolf, but also a fascinating and haunting parable.

Thurber, James. "The Little Girl and the Wolf." In *Fables of Our Times*. New York: Harper & Row, 1940.
  The character in this fable is a modern-day little girl with things in her basket for today's walk through the woods.

Yolen, Jane. "Wolf Child," and "Happy Dens; or, A Day in the Old Wolves' Home." In *The Faery Flag*. New York: Orchard Books, 1989.
  This collection of stories and poems gathers familiar fairy tales and items with ghost and supernatural themes.

Magazine and Newspaper Articles

Allen, Durward L., and L. David Mech. "Wolves Versus Moose on Isle Royale." *National Geographic* (February 1963): 200-219.
  Information and observations on the ten-year study to introduce wolves on Isle Royale National Park, Michigan.

Brandenburg, Jim. "White Wolf: Living with an Arctic Legend." *Reader's Digest* (March 1989): 126-32.
An exerpt from Brandenburg's book, with some observations on wolves in the wild.

Fitzgerald, Kevin. "The Wolf." *Colorado Outdoors* (September/October 1975): 13-16.
Background information on the wolf and some suggestions for the future.

George, Jean. "Animals Are Only Human." *Reader's Digest* (November 1973): 203-7.
In light of fascinating behavioral studies of some of the higher animal species, it is now not unscientific to attribute some human feelings and characteristics to animals. This author tells why.

Rau, Ron. "Showdown on the Tundra." *Reader's Digest* (February 1976): 147-50.
The author details an encounter with a wolf on the tundra of Alaska.

Robbins, Jim. "World of Wolves." *The Denver Post* (June 21, 1992): "Contemporary," pp. 12-14.
Describes the activities of a wildlife biologist researching the habits of the gray wolf in Montana with the hope that people will help in their start toward recovery.

Tomkies, Richard. "Bobo, A Wolf in the House." *Reader's Digest* (July 1975): 192-220.
The story of a family that has a full-grown wolf living with them. It regarded the family as a wolf pack and the family members had to live by the pack law themselves.

Williams, Ted. "Bringing Back the Beasts of Lore." *Modern Maturity* (June/July 1988): 44-51.
A mini-course on the reintroduction of the wolf to Isle Royale.

Films and Recordings

Fox, Michael W. "The Music of the Canids." A Science Year Recording, Field Enterprises, 1973.
An authority on dogs and their wild cousins narrates a recording on the often-musical sounds canids make. Included on the record are wolf howls.

How Animals Speak. (Film) McGraw-Hill, 1973.

Mason, Bill. *Cry of the Wild*. (Film) National Film Board of Canada, 1971.

———. *Death of a Legend*. (Film) National Film Board of Canada, 1971.

We Called Them Brother. (Film) Narrated by Jimmy Stewart, San Diego Zoo, 1975.

Bears

THE PEASANT AND THE BEAR

A Russian Folktale

 peasant was plowing a field one day when a bear came out of the woods and said to him, "Peasant, I will break your spindly bones."

"No, do not harm me, please. I am sowing turnips here and I will make a promise to you. I will take only the roots for myself and give you all of the tops. Only, don't break my weary bones."

"So be it!" said the bear, "but if you cheat me, do not dare to come into my forest for wood or anything else." Having said this, the bear shambled off back into the woods.

The days passed until it was time to harvest the crops. As the peasant was digging the bear came out of the thicket. "Now, peasant, let us share as you promised!" demanded the bear.

"Very well, little bear. I will bring you all of the tops." The peasant loaded a cart full of leaves and stalks and took them to the bear. The bear was quite satisfied that the peasant had kept his word and shared honestly. Then the peasant loaded his turnips onto a cart and prepared to drive to town to sell them.

The bear saw what the peasant was doing, so he came up to him and asked, "Peasant, where are you going?"

"I am going to town, little bear, to sell my roots," replied the peasant.

Let me taste one of those roots in your cart," said the puzzled bear. The peasant gave him a turnip. As soon as the bear chewed, crunched, and ate it, he began to roar, "Aha, you have cheated me, peasant. Your roots are sweet. Do not dare to come into the forest for wood or anything else. I will tear you to pieces!"

The peasant returned from town and for days things were quite normal except that he had no wood to burn. He was fearful of going into the forest, knowing the anger of the bear, so he burned his shelves. He burned his benches. Then he burned his wooden tubs and barrels. Still, in the end there was nothing else for him to do but to go into the forest and get some wood. He drove his cart very quietly and suddenly, from somewhere, a fox came running. "Why do you walk on tiptoe and drive your cart so quietly, little peasant?" the fox asked.

"I am very afraid of the bear. He is angry with me and has threatened to tear me into little pieces," the peasant replied.

"Don't fear the bear," said the fox. "Chop your wood and I will make noises like those the hunters make. If the bear asks what is happening, tell him that it is a bear and wolf hunt."

The peasant began to cut wood. Suddenly the bear rushed toward him, crying, "Hey, old man, what is this noise? What are you doing?"

"It is a bear and wolf hunt," said the peasant in a quivery voice.

"Oh, little peasant, put me in your cart, cover me with wood, and tie me with a rope. The hunters will think that I am a log," ordered the bear.

The peasant did as the bear asked. He helped the bear crawl into the cart, tied him with a rope, and then hit the bear on the head with the butt end of his axe until the bear was dead.

The fox came and looked around. "Where is the bear?" he asked.

"He is dead," answered the breathless peasant.

"Well, little peasant, now you must treat me to something for all of my help," said the fox, rubbing his paws in glee.

"Yes, indeed, little fox. Come to my house and I shall indeed treat you," sang the peasant. The peasant drove the cart with the bear and wood in it while the fox ran ahead of him. When the peasant was close to his house, he whistled to his dogs and set them on the fox.

The fox ran to the woods, jumped into a hole to hide, and mumbled, "Oh, little eyes, what did you do while I was running?"

"Oh, little fox, we saw to it that you did not stumble," replied the eyes.

"Oh, little ears, what did you do?" asked the fox.

"We listened all the time to hear whether the hounds were far behind," answered the ears.

"And you, tail, what did you do?" queried the fox.

"I," said the tail, "threw myself between your legs to entangle you so that you would fall and be torn to pieces by the dogs."

"Aha, you scoundrel! Let the dogs eat you then!" ordered the fox. He stuck his tail out of the hole. "Eat the fox's tail, dogs!" he screamed.

The hounds dragged the fox out of the hole by the tail and finished him off with howls of victory.

So does it often happen that because of the tail, the head perishes.

►●◄

FOLKLORE

Bear worship is a most ancient practice. Archaeological sites in Germany provide clear evidence of ceremony and cultic ritual associated with the bear hunt and the veneration of cave bears so killed. Vestiges of ancient Germanic bear worship still exist, although now they are relegated to folk festivals and seasonal holidays. The man dressed in a bearskin as the *Fastnacht* (Shrovetide) bear in German villages dances with all the village maidens and begs from house to house for money to buy beer. It was considered lucky to meet a bear.

Norwegians once believed that Finns and Lapps were magicians who could transform themselves into bears. That differs from the Finnish belief that bears are sacred, immortal animals. The bear is called the "Dog of God" in Lapland. Native Americans also revered the bear and saw the grizzly bear as a symbol of great strength and stamina. To them it was traditionally a sign of a warrior's courage if he battled with a bear and emerged victorious. They also used the sign of a bear paw as a symbol of good fortune.

Scandinavians have said that the bear has the strength of ten and the wit of twelve men. Almost universally, the hunter who killed a bear had to formally beg the bear's pardon and bring its dead body home with elaborate ceremonies and mystic rites. There is a Scandinavian story of a white bear who carries away his children so that they may later help their mother when she sets out to find him. This is the common theme of a wife who has disobeyed her husband and her long, weary search for him.

The stars in the constellation Ursa Major were commonly identified with the bear in India, Greece, and North America, a Greek legend relates that originally the sky was made of soft glass, which touched the earth on both sides. When someone nailed a bearskin on it, the nails became stars. The tail of the bear is represented by the three bright stars that are also known as the handle of the Big Dipper. The Big Dipper is contained within the Ursa Major, or Big Bear, constellation. A source of particular wonder to the Greeks was the apparent reluctance of the Bear to wet its feet in the waters that girdled the earth. The Greek story of Callisto and Arcas explains why the Bear spends eternity circling far above the north horizon and is not able to enter the deep, green kingdom of the sea to rest, bathe, or even drink from the celestial ocean.

It is said that when the first European explorers came to the North American continent, and had learned to speak the language of the natives, they pointed up north one evening and said, "See those seven stars? They are the stars we call the Bear." The Native Americans agreed that those were their bear stars too. Although the Native American peoples recognized a bear in the Bear stars, they were too familiar with the anatomy of that animal to believe that the three curving stars in the handle of our Dipper could be its tail; the earthly bear has no tail to speak of. They explained the tail stars as three hunters, hot on the trail of the great beast. For more stories related to bears in the constellations, refer to the Livo and Rietz book in this chapter's bibliography.

The story of King Arthur of the Round Table is also interwoven with the history of the Great Bear. Arthur's name supposedly came from the Welsh words for bear, *arth*, and wonderful, *Uthyr*. The Bear stars were his special symbol, and some of his followers claimed that he was actually an incarnation of the spirit of the constellation. The shape of the famous Round Table might also have come from the conspicuous circle made by the swinging of the Bear's tail and the great arc it made.

The Ute people believe that their tribal ancestor was the bear. In folklore it is believed that if a bear goes into its den early, a long winter will follow. The dictionary has many bear references such as to *bearbaiting* (an old form of diversion in which dogs were made to torment a chained bear). The word *bugbear* may have come from England, where there was said to be a goblin bear.

DISCUSSION

Description

Bears are large, heavy mammals of the family *Ursidae* that eat any sort of food, have shaggy fur, and have very short tails. A medium-size bear stands about 3 feet (1 meter) high at the shoulders and weighs an average of about 300 pounds (136 kilograms). Larger bears may grow to stand more than 10 feet (3 meters) tall and may weigh 1,700 pounds (772 kilograms). Bears have short, powerful legs and long, heavy toenails. They walk flat on the soles of their feet and not on their toes, as dogs and cats do. This gives them a clumsy look, but they can run rapidly for short distances over either smooth or rocky ground. Many kinds of bears can climb trees swiftly and expertly. Their sense of smell is very keen and they also hear fairly well. Because of their small eyes, they see poorly.

There are several kinds of bears. Among them are the black bear, the grizzly bear, the Kodiak bear, the Alaskan brown bear, the polar bear, the Asian brown bear, the sloth bear and sun bear from southern Asia and the East Indies, the Atlas bear of Africa, and the South American spectacled bear of the Andes.

The North American black bear is one of the most common of the bears. This species of bear is sometimes referred to as the "clown of the woods." It is the smallest of all the North American bears. Most black bears are entirely black, but occasionally an individual animal will have a brown patch on the nose or a white patch on the chest. One branch of this species, called "cinnamon bears," have brown fur. Black bears spend much of the winter sleeping or hibernating and this is when their cubs are born. Cubs weigh only about half a pound (227 grams) at birth and are 7 to 9 inches (18 to 23 centimeters) long. Born blind and nearly hairless, their eyes stay closed for nearly a month. Cubs usually stay inside the den until they are about two months old. Bear cubs reach full growth in about two years. Black bears live from fifteen to twenty-five years.

The grizzly bear (*Ursus horribilis*) is much larger and heavier than the black bear. The grizzly can be brownish-yellow, gray (sometimes called "silvertips") or a reddish-brown or "cinnamon." It stands about 3.5 feet (1 meter) at the shoulders (on all fours) and weighs about 350 to 800 pounds (159 to 363 kilograms). Some have been recorded at 1,800 pounds (817 kilograms) standing 9 feet (2.7 meters) tall. Their claws are very long but blunt, so they seldom climb trees after they are fully grown. A grizzly bear can be distinguished from a black bear by its humped shoulders and its concave face, which gives it a "dished-in" look in contrast to the black bear's more rounded profile. Generally, grizzlies do not hibernate through the winter.

The Kodiak and Alaskan brown bears are closely related. (They are also related to the grizzlies.) They are the largest of all flesh-eating mammals living on land. Some Kodiak bears are dark brown while others are yellowish-brown. The Kodiak is the largest species of bear in the world.

The brown bear of Europe and Asia appears in many children's stories under the name *Bruin* (which means *brown*). The only kind of bear commonly found in India and Sri Lanka is the sloth bear or honey bear. Its hair is long and black. The sun bear is found in Malaya, Sumatra, and Borneo. It is only about 4 feet (1.2 meters) long, with black fur and a patch of white or orange hair on its chest.

Since the fur of bears is thickest in fall and winter, bears are killed at these times for their skins, which are often used for rugs and covers. Their fur is also used for trimming clothes and for making hats and coats.

Behavior

Even though brown bears are timid and playful, and are often raised as pets, kept in zoos, and trained for animal acts, they can make dangerous enemies. The bears seldom attack human beings unless they are wounded, are defending their young, or have been teased with offers of food. Brown bears spend much of the winter sleeping in snug shelters or dens within caves, hollow trees, hollows under stumps, crevices in rocks, or holes dug in the earth.

Grizzly bears are considered to be the most dangerous of all North American wild animals and are reputed to have savage dispositions.

Both the black bear and the grizzly bear are omnivores. That means they eat both animal and plant matter. Some of the foods they prefer include dead and rotting meat, deer, elk, rodents, insects, fruits, nuts, berries, and other parts of plants. They are also known as successful fishers and habitual honey snatchers.

Habitat

Bears are native to temperate and arctic zones. Polar bears of the far north are at home in icy waters. Since they are omnivores, they have adapted to the environment. Access to plants, fish, and animals for food seem to be their basic requirement for survival.

Historic Range

Bears were once quite common in North America, South America, Asia, Africa, Europe, and the East Indies. The sun bears of Malaya, Sumatra, and Borneo are found in rain forests. Grizzlies were once found from the Black Hills of South Dakota westward, and from Mexico to northern Alaska. Today, they are rarely seen except in the higher slopes of the Rocky Mountains and occasionally in Yellowstone Park.

Reasons for Endangerment and Attempts to Help

"The grizzly bear is vanishing so rapidly that without protection he is likely to become extinct. Fear of bears and prejudice against them is all too often taught and developed in childhood." For instance, parents hush their children by telling them, "Bears will get you if you are not good." Although this quotation could have been written last week, by a modern conservationist, it actually comes from a 1919 book by Enos Mills. He wrote this long before the National Park Service closed the garbage dumps in Yellowstone National Park, which were phased out between 1968 and 1971. These dumps had become important food sources for bears. The Craighead brothers (see resource bibliography, page 41) argued that hungry bears would cause problems and that the Park Service should provide food temporarily to help them adjust to the closing of the dumps. Unfortunately, they were right. As hungry bears became a threat to park visitors, park personnel stepped up "control actions." As a result, many bears died or were killed, and now many biologists fear that the grizzlies will dwindle in number until none are left. Some scientists estimate that as few as fifty grizzly females of breeding age remain in the Yellowstone area. Denali National Park in Alaska has developed a program to discourage grizzlies from coming into contact with people, which is far more enlightened and effective at protecting both bears and humans.

Bears in general are suffering from encroachment on their territory by humans and their domestic animals. Although the omnivorous bear can adapt to the presence of humans, and even flourish on the humans' cast-off food sources, humans do not tolerate the potential danger to property, pets, livestock, and person that bears pose. Thus, the bears are killed. It is amazing to trace the ancient worship of bears to today's attitude of fear toward and killing of the bears.

Efforts to help the bears seem to be disjointed, controversial, and not very appropriate. Spring bear hunts still occur in Colorado, which is just after the females have had their cubs. Not only does the female bear die, so do her cubs. Whenever there are confrontations between humans and bears, the bear always loses eventually. Although there have been attempts to relocate bears when they get too close to civilization, these efforts are not always successful, since many of the bears find their way back again.

The Teddy Bear

Over eighty years ago, when President Theodore Roosevelt went bear hunting, he and the guide spotted a cub. Roosevelt refused to shoot it because it was too little to defend itself. A newspaper artist, Cliff Berryman, drew a cartoon about it for the *Washington Post* in 1902. A candy store owner in Brooklyn, New York, Morris Michtom, saw the cartoon and he and his wife started making stuffed toy bears. They got approval from the president to use the name "Teddy" for their toys. Michtom later started the Ideal Toy Company. About the same time, in Germany, the Steiff toy company also began making stuffed bears. The bears were a great hit from the beginning. Other popular bears that can be found in toy shops are Winnie-the-Pooh, who is now over fifty years old, and Paddington Bear. Both of these bears were made very popular in children's books.

BEAR ACTIVITIES

Bears and the Environment

- Collect pictures of and articles about bears from newspapers and magazines for use in a variety of activities. Ask your librarian or library media specialist for help.

- Refer to the PROJECT WILD (see bibliography) materials on bears. These include "Bearly Born" that helps students identify similar survival needs of both black bear cubs and human babies. "What Bear Goes Where?" works with the identification of three species of bears and their habitats. "Polar Bears in Phoenix" examines problems for an animal moved from its natural environment to captivity. "How Many Bears Can Live in This Forest?" enables students to understand carrying capacity and its importance for wildlife and people. The last activity, "Smokey the Bear Said What?" explores positive and negative consequences of forest and range fires and the changes fire can make in ecosystems. (Contact your state Division of Wildlife for information on PROJECT WILD materials.)

- Develop a web for the topic of bears and the environment. (See the sample web on page 35 for some ideas.) Indicate categories of people such as rangers, economists, biologists, tourists, media, resort owners, environmentalists, theologians, historians, and tourist industry representatives. Read and discuss material on bears, their reintroduction to national parks, their relationship to people, their proximity to residents, and any other information available. Then mark the connections on the web as either positive or negative factors. Categorize the people on the web regarding their positive or negative feelings towards bears. Compare results and evaluate why some people might have different reactions on their lists. Evaluate the effect the introduction of the teddy bear and other stuffed toy bears might have had on the general perception of bears. Do these cuddly toys influence the feelings of children or parents? If students are experienced in debating, a debate on the reasons for positive or negative thinking could be developed. See figure 3.1 for a sample web.

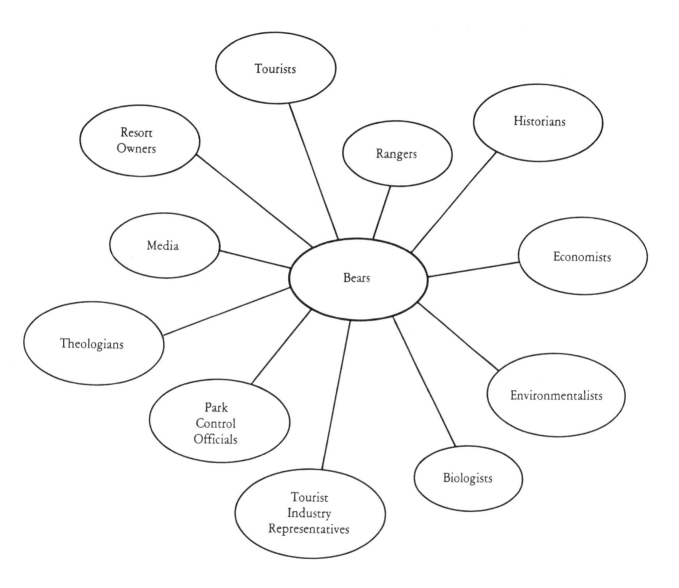

Fig. 3.1. Bear web.

- Find stories in literature or in magazines about true experiences with bears. If possible, interview someone who has had an experience with a bear.

- Research where bears are found. Are they found in your area? Make a map showing where bears can be found. Discuss safety rules for humans who enter bear territory. Make a chart of rules.

- How much does a bear eat in a day, week, or month? Create a graph displaying this information. Compare it to what you eat in the same period.

- Research phrases, similes, and metaphors such as "to bear something in mind," "to bear down," "to bear up," "to bring to bear," and "hungry as a bear." Where do these expressions come from? What do they mean?

Bears in the News

- Bears often make the news. On pages 38-40 appear reprints of three articles from newspapers—all about bears. In figure 3.2, page 37, a synopsis of an article discusses Yellowstone National Park and two populations that are sometimes in conflict—bears and people.

  1. Invite speakers to discuss the National Park Service's philosophy toward bears. Speakers from biology departments of local colleges and universities, U.S. Fish and Wildlife Service, or your state Division of Wildlife would be excellent resources.

  2. Find maps of Yellowstone Park and Denali National Park (Alaska). How far is Yellowstone or Denali from your home? How large are Yellowstone and Denali parks? Make a contour map of Yellowstone or Denali.

  3. Write to Yellowstone or Denali parks services or the Interagency Grizzly Bear Committee to collect more information on bears.

  4. Research the natural diet of the grizzly.

  5. Garbage dumps contain more than just food. Find out what other trash is in a dump (for example, styrofoam cups, plastic cutlery, etc.) and what threat it poses to bears.

  6. Plan a family trip to Yellowstone or Denali. Estimate expenses of camping, driving (mileage), and food.

  7. Graph the population changes of bears. Contact your state Division of Wildlife for sources and statistics.

  8. Graph visitation statistics to Yellowstone National Park or other national parks over a several-year period. Contact the National Park Service. Compare to bear population changes. Can you see any trends?

  9. Experts on bears stated that "about 95 percent of bears are intelligent and stay out of trouble." What characteristics would a smart bear display? Make a chart contrasting smart and not-so-smart bear behavior.

Declining Bear Population in Yellowstone

At a grizzly bear symposium held at Casper College in Casper, Wyoming, in 1984, opinions differed on what is causing a decline in the grizzly bear population in Yellowstone National Park. And opinions differed on what to do about it.

Two brothers, John and Frank Craighead, are among the world's foremost experts on the grizzly bear. Frank Craighead said he figured, "Forty-four percent of the grizzly bear population was lost in the years of the late '60s and '70s." They were particularly concerned that the female grizzly population had dropped dramatically and blamed "the destruction of ecocenters." *Ecocenters* is a term they used for the garbage dumps where the grizzly bears found most of their food. The National Park Service closed the dumps in 1967 because of new procedures handed down from the federal government.

The Craigheads wanted the government to provide supplemental feedings in hopes of promoting the bear population again. Some members of the Interagency Grizzly Bear Committee, a research committee studying the bear population in Yellowstone, disagreed with the Craigheads. They want to "allow the bear to pursue natural behavior patterns, such as breeding, feeding and resting without intrusion or disturbance of humans." Gary Brown, a committee member, said the committee has four objectives: "good information policy, elimination of unnatural food sources, the prompt removal of problem bears and the enforcement of regulations in Yellowstone."

Another committee member, Steve Mealy, said he trusts nature. "Give the species the benefit of a doubt and it will survive."

Despite their differing views, the Craigheads and the committee members admit that they have a lot of respect for one another. The Craigheads said in particular they wanted to clear up some "long-standing misconceptions about the controversy in Yellowstone." They said they did not advocate keeping the dumps open but wanted to have a gradual phasing out of the dumps. And they did not advocate reopening the dumps.

Fig. 3.2. Synopsis of an article printed in *The Denver Post* (April 29, 1984).

- In figure 3.3, page 38, the article "Grizzlies in Colorado—Again?" explores a plan to reintroduce the grizzly bear to the mountains of southwest Colorado.

  1. Correspond with officials on this topic and collect all the information you can find. Discuss and debate the pros and cons of this reintroduction plan. What are some of the problems? For addresses of officials, refer to the resource information section at the end of this book (page 163).

  2. How would people know whether grizzly bears still lived in Colorado? What signs would they look for?

  3. On a blank map of the United States, shade the mountain ranges being considered for reintroduction of the grizzly bear. Examine human population patterns in these areas. What are the implications?

Grizzlies in Colorado — again?

By Gary Gerhardt
Rocky Mountain News Staff Writer

The San Juan Mountains of Colorado may be the future home of grizzly bears.

The Interagency Grizzly Bear Committee is conducting hearings in Washington tomorrow to obtain public comment on a revised draft plan for reintroduction of the grizzly in the San Juans, the Cascade Mountains in Washington and the Bitterroot Range in Idaho and Montana.

The committee includes members of the U.S. Fish and Wildlife Service, National Forest Service and game managers from Montana, Wyoming and Idaho.

John Green, administrative secretary of the committee, said yesterday the San Juans were added to the list at the last minute. It's

doubtful any "on ground" evaluation will take place before 1992 at the earliest, he said.

"We decided to add the San Juans to the Bitterroot and Cascades after receiving letters from Tony Povilitis and others saying they have evidence grizzly may still exist in southern Colorado," Green said.

Povilitis, a senior scientist for the Humane Society of the United States, spent last summer in the Wolf Creek Pass area looking for grizzlies and believes he found evidence that a few of the great bears may still be roaming the back country of the state.

He said four people, including an outfitter, reported seeing grizzlies, tracks or other signs in the San Juans in recent years and asked Colorado Division of Wildlife officials to ban hunting in the area this big-game season.

The division turned down Povilitis' request, but it did ask hunters to report any possible sighting or other evidence that might confirm the presence of grizzly bears.

Extensive surveys in the early 1980s failed to find any grizzlies in Colorado, although researchers say that doesn't rule out the possibility some may remain in remote areas.

The last known grizzly in Colorado died in 1979 after attacking an outfitter a few miles southwest of Wolf Creek Pass.

The sighting was a surprise because it was generally believed grizzlies in Colorado had been killed off 30 years earlier.

Fig. 3.3. *Rocky Mountain News* (November 14, 1990): 10. Reprinted with permission of the *Rocky Mountain News*.

- In figure 3.4 the article, "Lost Hunter Spooked Bear with Camera," is a true story about one man's adventure with a bear and how he coped with a dangerous situation.

  1. Describe the weather patterns in the mountains at this time of year. Contact your local weather bureau for information.

  2. What is hypothermia? What are its causes, prevention, and treatment? How would you prepare for avoiding it?

  3. What would you pack for a five-day trip in the mountains?

  4. Plan a rescue operation in bear country. How would you safely search for and rescue a wounded person?

5. Imagine you have been lost for five days in heavily populated bear territory. Keep a journal recording your experiences, thoughts, and observations. What are some of the bear behavior patterns you might expect if you were in such a situation? What supplies would be most useful to you?

6. If you could interview the man in the article, what would you ask him?

7. Make a commercial for the batteries in his camera.

Lost hunter spooked bear with camera

By Gary Gerhardt

Rocky Mountain News Staff Writer

A flashing camera strobe light was a lost Maryland hunter's only defense against a black bear that trapped him in a tree last weekend.

Bob Wiehr, who was caught in a blinding snowstorm and spent four below-freezing nights lost before being rescued Tuesday, said he kept flashing the strobe at the bear until it finally wandered away.

"I then saw somebody had put meat — bait — up in that tree. It would have been the one I chose to climb," he said with a laugh yesterday from his bed in Gunnison Valley Hospital, where he's recovering from frostbitten feet.

A carpenter in Bryan Road, Md., Wiehr, 44, is a Vietnam veteran who served two tours with the Marine Corps.

"I just kept telling myself, 'Don't work harder, work smarter,' and was able to keep my panic in check," he said.

Wiehr and three Maryland friends set up camp in the canyon-cut high country west of Gunnison Friday, a day before the season opened, and set out to scout for elk.

"I was wearing thermal long-johns, thermal boots, wool and cotton socks, a sweatshirt and vest," he said. "I had a canteen with water, but no food."

Because they were scouting, not hunting, none of the men carried weapons, Wiehr said. "All I had was sunglasses, a comb, pen, knife and camera."

Making his swing around the mountainside, Wiehr found truth in the old Colorado axiom: If you don't like the weather, wait a minute; it'll change.

"It was so beautiful when we went out, but I've never seen weather change so fast," he said.

Light snow started falling, then suddenly Wiehr was in a swirling storm that dumped a foot of snow.

He misjudged where camp was — later realizing he missed it by less than a quarter-mile — and soon realized he was lost.

Wiehr tried to build a fire, but his disposable lighter failed.

"That's when I climbed the tree and saw the bear," he said.

Each night, fearing attack by animals, he lashed himself into a tree with quarter-inch cord.

"I'm not a religious man, but I do remember thinking about Job and all the problems he had," Wiehr said. "And at night, I'd think about my kids." Wiehr has a son, 16, and daughter, 14, living in Maryland with his ex-wife.

On the third night, he began to suffer hypothermia.

"My clothes were wet. I couldn't get them dry, and I just had to keep getting mad at myself whenever I felt panic coming on."

During the days, he watched as helicopters flew over the area, sometimes coming within 500 yards of him, but the pilots didn't see the flash from his camera.

"There was a point where I had to admit to myself that this might be the end," he said. "I had plenty of water, but no food and couldn't get warm."

Then, as he stumbled along a ridge, he looked up to see Lowell Soleshee, an Oregon hunter, across a small gully.

"He asked me how I was doing, and I told him I'd been without food for five days, and he said, 'Oh, so you're the guy we've been looking for, huh?'"

Six hours later, a Gunnison County sheriff's rescue team had Wiehr on his way to the hospital.

Despite his experience, Wiehr said he would be back to hunt.

"Why not. I know that whole mountain now," he said, laughing.

Fig. 3.4. *Rocky Mountain News* (October 25, 1990): 10. Reprinted with permission of the *Rocky Mountain News*.

- In figure 3.5 the article, "Boulder Bear Back, Can Stay If He Behaves," is about a bear with a problem with people.

  1. Locate on a map where this story takes place.

  2. Discuss if it is a good idea to leave this bear where he is. Collect other stories showing human/wildlife conflict.

  3. Brainstorm other problems that might result from having the bear stay.

  4. Tell the story of what is happening from the bear's point of view. Trace the bear's route from Ft. Collins to Boulder, Colorado. Why do you think it returned to Boulder? What problems are associated with moving it? (You might want to read *Blueberries for Sal* by Robert McCloskey, see page 42.)

Boulder bear back, can stay if he behaves

By Kevin McCullen

Rocky Mountain News Boulder Bureau

BOULDER — The No. 9 bear is back in Boulder, where he can stay unless he causes trouble.

Wildlife officials have no plans to trap and relocate the young black bear, which is feasting on chokecherries, fruit from orchards and goodies in garbage cans around homes hugging the foothills near Chautauqua Park.

But should he begin to behave aggressively toward humans, the Colorado Division of Wildlife Resources may have no choice but to destroy the animal.

"He's a nuisance in some folks' minds, there's no doubt about it," district wildlife manager Kristi Coughlon said yesterday. "If it were the middle of the summer, we'd trap and relocate him because he is coming into people's back yards. But we won't risk public safety. If we have to remove

him at this point of the year, more than likely we'd have to put him down."

In August, the 100-pound bear surprised a Boulder man on Enchantment Mesa and chased him after he ran. Hikers and picnickers also spotted the 2-year-old bear near Chautauqua Park.

Coughlon tranquilized the bear, and wildlife officials put a purple ear tag marked No. 9 on the animal and moved him to an area west of Fort Collins. Coughlon estimated the distance at over 100 air miles.

But he returned to Boulder. And last week, the bear drifted into a residential area adjacent to the foothills. He was tranquilized and removed again to the foothills.

"There's been a good berry crop this year and that attracts

bears," Coughlon said. "They can follow the berries in draws all the way into town."

Wildlife officials hope the bear avoids humans and pets until it hibernates sometime during the next month. Coughlon said biologists will trap and relocate the bear next spring after it emerges from its winter rest.

"If we were to trap him and move him now, chances are he wouldn't make it to the spring," she said. "He'd have to adjust to a new area, where there probably would be other bears he'd have to compete with, and he'd be trying to adjust to this new area at a time when he's supposed to be storing up fat for the winter."

Fig. 3.5. *Rocky Mountain News* (October 28, 1990): 36. Reprinted with permission of the *Rocky Mountain News*.

RESOURCE BIBLIOGRAPHY

Browne, Anthony. *Bear Hunt*. New York: Doubleday, 1990.
Little Bear, with his pencil, is out for a jaunt in his jungle. Unfortunately, two hunters are out to capture Bear, with a variety of industrious schemes, but Bear manages to foil their strategies. Using his magic pencil, Bear draws his way out of each danger. Browne has two other books about Bear and his pencil: *The Little Bear Book* and *Bear Goes to Town*.

Calabro, Marian. *Operation Grizzly Bear*. New York: Four Winds Press, 1989.
Calabro describes the twelve-year study of grizzly bears done by Frank and John Craighead in Yellowstone National Park, during which their use of the radio-tracking collar and other innovations added to the scope of human knowledge about the grizzly.

Craighead, Frank C., Jr. *Track of the Grizzly*. San Francisco, Calif.: Sierra Club Books, 1979.
For thirteen years, Frank and his twin brother John tracked hundreds of grizzlies to discover these bears' social organization and seasonal movements, their breeding and feeding habits, and their life spans. This book points up the shortcomings of America's current system of wildlife management for the greatest omnivore in our hemisphere.

Czernecki, Stefan, and Timothy Rhodes. *Bear in the Sky*. New York: Sterling, 1990.
Told in the tradition of the ancient classic fables and legends about the constellations, *Bear in the Sky* is about a great brown bear who loves to dance to the tunes of his gypsy musician friends. A willful princess tries to keep the bear in a castle tower for her own selfish amusement, but the bear escapes and gets a long tail in the process.

Ford, Barbara. *Black Bear, the Spirit of the Wilderness*. Boston: Houghton Mifflin, 1981.
This book, illustrated with black-and-white photographs, discusses the black bear, North America's smallest bear, the research being done on it, and our responsibility for ensuring its future.

George, Jean Craighead. *The Grizzly Bear with the Golden Ears*. New York: Harper & Row, 1982.
Noted author Jean Craighead George is the sister of the Craighead brothers, who researched the grizzly bears in Yellowstone Park. This family is a clear example of people who have been raised to respect nature and all its creatures. In Ms. George's book, a grizzly bear who bluffs rather than hunts for her food learns an important lesson. This is a suspenseful tale presented through a graceful, poetic text.

Goldstein, Bobbye S. *Bear in Mind*. Illustrated by William Pene Du Bois. New York: Viking Kestrel, 1989.
Goldstein has given us a delightful illustrated collection of poems, ballads, limericks, and rhymes about bears.

Jonas, Ann. *Two Bear Cubs*. New York: Greenwillow, 1982.
Two adventurous cubs love to wander, but when frightened, appreciate having their mother close by.

Kesey, Ken. *Little Tricker the Squirrel Meets Big Double the Bear*. Illustrated by Barry Moser. New York: Viking, 1990.
Little Tricker the squirrel watches as Big Double the bear terrorizes the forest animals one by one, but then Little Tricker gets revenge.

Livo, Norma J., and Sandra Rietz. *Storytelling Folklore Sourcebook*. Englewood, Colo.: Libraries Unlimited, 1991.
This is a collection of folklore ideas and examples to show how folklore items can be incorporated into storytelling. The chapter on stars includes a section on the Bear constellation.

Marshall, James. *Goldilocks and the Three Bears*. New York: Dial, 1988.
This version is full of humorous details, such as a bear rug on the floor, and a refrain that begs for listener/reader participation.

McCloskey, Robert. *Blueberries for Sal*. New York: Viking, 1948.
Sal gets home safely after following a bear in the blueberry patch.

McClung, Robert M. *Major, the Story of a Black Bear*. Hamden, Conn.: Linnet, 1988.
The author demonstrates a respect for and interest in the black bear.

_____. *Samson, Last of the California Grizzlies*. New York: Morrow, 1973.
The title tells it all.

_____. *The True Adventures of Grizzly Adams*. New York: Morrow, 1985.
A look at a famous character of American frontier history.

Mikaelsen, Ben. *Rescue Josh McGuire*. New York: Hyperion, 1991.
Thirteen-year-old Josh runs away to the mountains of Montana with an orphaned bear cub destined for laboratory testing. They both must fight for their lives.

Mills, Enos A. *The Grizzly*. New York: Ballantine, 1919.
Enos Mills is credited as being the creator of Glacier and Rocky Mountain national parks. His observations and intimate knowledge of this magnificent beast have never been equalled. For a lifetime he trailed grizzlies, without a gun, across the ranges, plateaus, and passes of the Rocky Mountains. Observing without interfering, he caught unusual glimpses of their way of life and his stories add much to our understanding of the grizzly. Mills said, "I would give the grizzly first place in the animal world for brain power. Instinct the grizzly has, but he also has the ability to reason." Truly a classic study of animal behavior.

Patent, Dorothy Hinshaw. *The Way of the Grizzly*. Illustrated by William Munoz. New York: Clarion, 1987.
The Way of the Grizzly describes through text and illustrations the physical characteristics, habits, and natural environment of the grizzly bear and the threats humans pose to the bears' survival.

Petterssan, Bertil. *In the Bear's Forest*. Translated by Steven T. Murry from Swedish. Stockholm, Sweden: Ribén & Sjögren, 1991. (Marketed in the United States by Farrar, Straus & Giroux.)

PROJECT WILD. Boulder, Colo.: Western Regional Environmental Education Council, 1986.
PROJECT WILD is an interdisciplinary, supplementary environmental and conservation education program for educators of kindergarten through high-school-age young people.

Riddell, Chris. *The Bear Dance*. New York: Simon and Schuster, 1990.
When Jack Frost brings gray winter to a forest where it is always summer, a young girl brings sunlight back by engaging Mr. Frost in a vigorous Bear Dance.

Rojankovsky, Feodor. *The Three Bears*. Racine, Wis.: Golden Press, 1980.
This edition is the fortieth printing of the 1948 Rojankovsky classic.

Ryder, Joanne. *The Bear on the Moon*. Illustrated by Carol Lacy. New York: Morrow, 1991.
An original story of how the Arctic world began and how the great white bears came to live on ice and snow.

Schindler, Regine. *The Bear's Cave*. Illustrated by Sita Jucker. New York: Dutton, 1990.
Rabbit and Mouse spend the winter with Bear in his cave, telling him wonderful but untrue stories of how they can fly and the things they have seen.

Stevens, Janet. *Goldilocks and the Three Bears*. New York: Holiday House, 1986.
This version of the story of the little girl who wanders by the home of the three bears, goes inside, helps herself to food, and falls asleep, is a good one for comparison with the Rojankovsky book.

Turkle, Brinton. *Deep in the Forest*. New York: Dutton, 1976.
This wordless book is a twist on the familiar story of Goldilocks and the three bears. The art is worthy of study as to how it advances the story and, of course, all readers can create their own stories from the pictures.

Elephants

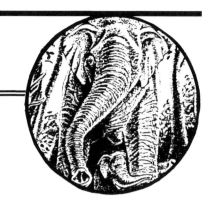

THE ELEPHANTS AND THE LION

A Chinese Folktale

he huntsman of Kuang-si was out in the fields one bright day. On this day the hunter was not having good luck. Animals managed to avoid his arrows and he covered much ground unsuccessfully looking for game. In the warmth of the sun, he grew tired, so he found a shady tree, sat down and leaned up against it, put his bow and arrows on the ground close beside him, and fell fast asleep.

As he slumbered, he dreamed of exciting hunts where his arrows were true on the mark and his bravery was the envy of all. While he slept, an elephant came along, coiled its trunk around the sleeping man, and carried him off. The bouncing motion of the lumbering elephant woke the hunter up. He was terrified by the situation in which he found himself and felt that he was a dead man. He was saddened by the realization that his dreams would not come true, that he would not live to become an old, brave hunter. Surprisingly, he felt his bow and arrows held fast in his hand, but they were of no use because the elephant's trunk was wrapped completely around him and the elephant was carrying him like a piece of timber.

Before long, though, the elephant put the hunter down at the foot of a tall tree. To the hunter's amazement, the elephant then called to a whole herd of other elephants, who crowded around the frightened hunter and seemed to ask for his help. The elephant who had taken him from his sleep went over to the tree and knelt down. It looked up into the branches of the tree and then looked down at the hunter. After the elephant had done this numerous times, the hunter came to the conclusion that the elephant was asking for his help. What was happening that all the elephants seemed to be asking him for help?

Once more gathering his courage, the man walked over to the elephant and climbed on its back. He then caught a branch of the tree and

45

clambered from branch to branch to the very topmost branch of the tree. He had no idea what was expected of him, but there he was. As he sat there up in his perch, he saw a sleek lion slinking toward the frightened herd of elephants. The lion had picked out one fat elephant from among the others in the herd and it seemed to the hunter that the lion was about to attack it. All the other elephants just stood there trembling, looking up at the top of the tree and shaking. They did not run away, but they all looked so wistful that the man drew his sharpest arrow from his quiver and shot the lion. His arrow was swift, true, and deadly.

Around the dead lion, all the elephants below bowed and gave obeisance to the hunter. Their gratitude was obvious. The hunter scurried down the trunk of the tree. When he got near the last branch, there was his elephant standing and waiting for him to climb down on its back. When he hesitated, the elephant gently tugged and pulled on his clothes. After he landed carefully on the elephant's back, the elephant moved carefully away from the tree. It traveled to a place where it circled and circled, until it seemed the elephant had found the spot it was looking for. It scratched the ground with its big foot and uncovered a huge pile of old elephant tusks. The elephant had brought the hunter to the burial ground of the elephants!

Seeing this, the hunter jumped off the animal's back and gathered all the tusks into a bundle. When he was done, the elephant once more wrapped its trunk around the hunter and placed him on its back. They traveled to a spot near the hunter's home and then the elephant let him down to the earth.

That night the mighty hunter had stories to tell that people almost refused to believe, but he had a vast number of tusks to prove his tales.

▶●◀

FOLKLORE

In ancient India, the elephant signified the god consort and represented his powerful sexual energy and potency. The virgin goddess of Chinese, Indian, and Greek mythologies is impregnated by the god in the form of a sacred elephant and subsequently gives birth to the sacrifice hero, the enlightened one. Ganesha, the name of the Indian elephant god, is the precursor of Yahweh's title "Lord of Hosts." Early Jewish mercenaries of the fifth century B.C. worshipped the elephant. Because of its mythological connection to gods and their sexual capabilities, the elephant's tusks continued to be prized well into the Middle Ages. An *oliphant* or war horn made of an elephant's tusk was thought to possess remarkable magical properties.

In folklore, the elephant is characterized as wise, patient, affectionate, grateful, of pleasant disposition, and generous with help. It is a symbol of temperance, eternity, and sovereignty. In Indian mythology, the world is supported by eight elephants. The world elephant Airavata was produced by the churning of the primeval ocean. Getting on an elephant's back will bring good fortune, and elephants in general are considered to be good luck. It is said that the breath of the elephant will draw a snake from its hole. As a token of success and good fortune, carry a hair taken from the tail of an elephant or elephant teeth and bones.

White elephants were considered to have the magical power of producing clouds. In India, it was once believed that the first elephants were milk-white, had large wings, and flew about in the sky.

The King of Siam used to make a present of a white elephant to courtiers whom he wished to ruin. Because such elephants were sacred and as such were not to be worked, their possession and upkeep was tremendously expensive. This is the origin of our term *white elephant* for an unwanted item. Today we have fun exchanging gifts considered to be white elephants, but originally it was a very serious gift that could have heavy financial consequences for the new owner.

Queen Maya of Nepal had a dream that a white elephant with six tusks had entered her body. White stood for humility and the number six was sacred because it corresponds to the six dimensions of space: upward, downward, forward, backward, left, and right. Soothsayers predicted that the queen would bear a son who would become either the ruler of the world or the savior of mankind. This foretold the birth of Gautama Buddha.

Another common folk belief is that an elephant never forgets. While this is a slight exaggeration, the elephant does have unusual ability to remember very complicated tasks it has been taught. To a surprising degree, elephants are also capable of understanding human speech, not just the sounds but the actual meaning of words. These skills put the elephant among the more intelligent animals after humans.

DISCUSSION

Description

Elephants are the largest of the land animals and are descendants of the prehistoric woolly mammoth, which died out approximately 10,000 years ago. Today there are two different kinds of elephants, the Asiatic (*Elephas maximus*) and the African (*Loxodonta africana*). These two species are all that remain of more than 600 different kinds of elephants that have inhabited the earth.

It is quite easy to differentiate the Asiatic elephant from the African. Asiatic elephants have smaller ears, smooth hides, high foreheads, and two prominent bumps on their foreheads. They have hump-type arched backs. Usually only the males have tusks. African elephants are generally larger and have very large, fan-like ears and rough skins. Both males and females have tusks. Their backs also arch, but in more of a swayback than the Asiatics'. An elephant calf at birth weighs about 200 pounds (90.8 kilograms). Elephants in India may live to be seventy or eighty years old.

Behavior

Elephants grow six sets of teeth during their lifetime. This is an adaptation to the coarseness of the wide variety of foods they eat. When its last set of teeth is worn down, the elephant can no longer chew food, so it dies. Elephants use their flexible, prehensile trunks to pick up grass and to reach high into treetops. Their tusks are used to plow up the ground during the search for food. The tusks are also useful for getting into the soft cores of tree branches and for digging for water in dry riverbeds.

Elephants have been recorded as walking 300 miles (483 kilometers) in search of food and water. Their normal speed is 4 to 5 miles (6.4 to 8 kilometers) per hour, but they have been known to run as fast as 24 miles (38.6 kilometers) per hour for short distances.

Elephants love water and will bathe several times a day, in addition to drinking large amounts, if water is available. Their water consumption is huge; one estimate places the amount at 15,500 gallons (58.9 kiloliters) per year per elephant. They also spray dust over themselves to keep insects from biting, and sometimes they cover themselves completely with mud.

Elephant families are very close-knit and the young are well cared for. Elephants make a variety of sounds, including screaming, trumpeting, grunting, purring, and rumbling. Their trunks magnify all these sounds.

Asiatic elephants have been used as work animals for thousands of years. They are still used in southern Asia to help clear forests, for heavy labor, and for pushing and carrying things and people. Military history documents the use of elephants as living "tanks" in war, in which they were used as much to frighten and confound the enemy as for their ability to transport burdens and people. African elephants have not been used as work animals to any great extent and have the reputation of being much harder to tame or train than their Asiatic counterparts.

Elephants have been part of circuses for at least 2,000 years. Jumbo was probably the most famous of circus animals. Jumbo, who stood 11 feet (3.4 meters) tall at his shoulder, may have been the largest elephant ever held in captivity. Elephants are also popular as zoo exhibit animals.

Habitat

Elephants need broad expanses of territory to find enough food to survive. Asiatic elephants live mostly in forests and prefer a diet of tree and bush foliage, along with a little grass. African elephants' primary food is grass, which makes up 90 percent of their diet, although they also eat tree bark and fruit. Because of their enormous water needs, they must live near or travel to water holes that can sustain an entire herd.

Historic Range

The elephant formerly ranged throughout Asia, Africa, and North America. Remains of woolly mammoths have been found frozen in ice in Siberia and Alaska, but these elephant ancestors became extinct about 10,000 years ago. Today, elephant populations are found only in central Africa and southeast Asia. Hunters killed the last elephants in northern Africa more than 1,200 years ago and elephants disappeared from southern Africa about 80 years ago. The map in figure 4.1 shows current elephant ranges.

Reasons for Endangerment and Attempts to Help

The lumbering beasts of the African savannah in particular are in critical danger. Poachers have killed elephants by the tens of thousands for the "white gold" ivory of their tusks. Elephant ivory, which is used for carvings, jewelry, scrimshaw, piano keys, and other ornaments and trinkets, is highly prized, with a single tusk bringing thousands of dollars in both the legal and illegal ivory markets.

Just a decade ago there were more than a million elephants in Africa; now there are, by many estimates, less than half that number. In Asia, the wild population may be as few as 25,000. The killing of the elephants endangers not only the elephants but also dozens of other species, such as wildebeest and antelope, whose open-grassland habitats are created and maintained when elephants eat their way through a jungle.

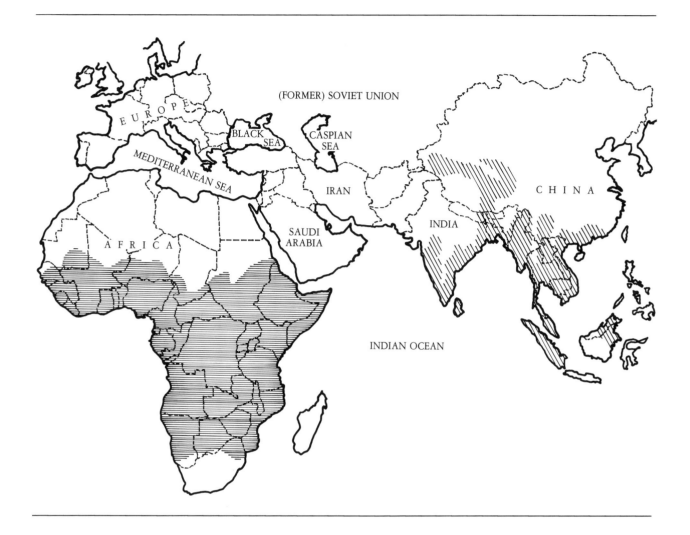

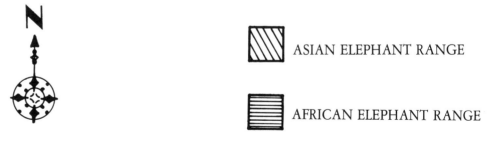

ASIAN ELEPHANT RANGE

AFRICAN ELEPHANT RANGE

0   1000   2000 mi.

0   1000 2000 km.

Fig. 4.1.

Official programs to help the elephant maintain its precarious foothold on existence include strict limits on ivory sales and aggressive actions against poachers. The government of Kenya, a country that has seen its elephant population decrease by 70 percent in the last ten years, pursues illegal hunters with new trucks, automatic weapons, aircraft surveillance, and orders to shoot to kill poachers on sight. However, when a single tusk can bring a poacher the equivalent of an average Kenyan's yearly wages, poaching will most likely continue. The better solution seems to be controlling the markets for ivory. Countries continue to petition that elephants and rhinoceroses be removed from the endangered list so that the ivory can be harvested; however, the Convention on International Trade in Endangered Species (CITES) is expected to agree on a complete ban on ivory sales in the United States, the nations of Europe, and many other countries. Japan, one of the world's largest importers of ivory, has made a commitment to stricter controls and to being more scrupulous in purchasing ivory only from legal sources.

Conservationists who insisted that a complete ban on ivory sales was the only way to protect the elephant may soon get their wish. In 1991, Japanese researchers, spurred by international treaties banning trade in ivory products, invented a test-tube "ivory" made from eggs and milk. When the price of ivory plummeted from twenty dollars a pound to two dollars a pound, poaching became too risky for the payoff and people stopped killing the elephants.[1]

Despite this progress, elephants in both Africa and Asia still face pressure from ever-increasing human encroachment into their habitats. With less and less land available for forage, added to the natural danger of extended drought, the reduced elephant populations may not be able to endure.

ELEPHANT ACTIVITIES

- Compare the Chinese story at the beginning of this elephant section with the story of "Sinbad's Seventh Voyage—The Elephant Hunt" from Olcott's collection of Arabian Nights tales (see resource bibliography, page 51). This story, as told by Sheherazade, is a variation on the Chinese one.

- Find the book *8,000 Stones* by Diane Wolkstein or the story "8,000 Stones" from *Pebbles from a Broken Jar: Fables and Hero Stories from Old China* by Frances Alexander. Use this story, which is one of resourcefulness, to develop a readers' theatre script. The Chinese governor wants to find out how much a gift elephant weighs so he can impress the Satrap from India who sent it to him. All the governor's advisers fail and it is up to the governor's clever young son to solve the problem.

- Read Kipling's "The Elephant's Child." Create and tell another story explaining why the elephant has big ears, tusks, etc.

- If possible, go to the zoo and observe the elephants there. In a notebook, record the behaviors of the elephants. Compare notebooks and list the behaviors recorded. Were there any differences?

- While at the zoo, sketch the elephants. What kind of elephants are in that zoo? Asian? African?

- Interview someone at the zoo to discover where the elephants came from and how they got to the zoo.

- Ask a librarian for books and stories about elephants. What activities can you develop from information and ideas found in these sources?

- Make elephant masks. Use these masks while performing a song, dance, or poem you have written.

- Write a rap song about elephants. Perform it for someone.

- Walt Disney created an elephant character called "Dumbo" who is featured in books and film. Either read one of the books or view the film and keep a list of things that are factual and another list of things that are fantasy.

NOTES

1. Richard Leakey, presentation at Denver Museum of Natural History, August 1991.

RESOURCE BIBLIOGRAPHY

Books

Alexander, Frances. "8,000 Stones." In *Pebbles from a Broken Jar: Fables and Hero Stories from Old China*, 11-19. Indianapolis, Ind.: Bobbs-Merrill, 1963, 1967.
Illustrated with papercuts by children.

Kennaway, Adrienne. *Little Elephant's Walk*. New York: HarperCollins, 1991.
Little Elephant roams over the plains and through the forests of Africa and sees a lion, a giraffe, an aardvark, and many other animals.

Kipling, Rudyard. *The Elephant's Child*. Adapted by Emily Bolam. New York: Dutton, 1992.
This is a story of how the elephant got its long trunk.

Kunkel, Richard. *Elephants*. New York: Harry N. Abrams, 1982.
A coffee-table book of photographs and essays on elephants.

Lobel, Arnold. *Uncle Elephant*. New York: Harper & Row, 1981.
Uncle Elephant takes care of his nephew when the young elephant's parents are lost at sea.

McClung, Robert M. *America's First Elephant*. Illustrated by Marilyn Janovitz. New York: Morrow Junior Books, 1991.
A female elephant from Bengal was brought to America in 1795. She was the first elephant to come to America. She toured the country and even met President Washington.

Olcott, Frances Jenkins, ed. *Tales from the Arabian Nights*. Racine, Wis.: Whitman, 1966.
This collection includes "Sinbad's Seventh Voyage — The Elephant Hunt."

Patent, Dorothy Hinshaw. *African Elephants, Giants of the Land*. Photographs by Oria Doublas-Hamilton. New York: Holiday House, 1991.
Patent describes the physical characteristics, behavior, feeding, family life, and habitat of the African elephant.

Smucker, Barbara. *Incredible Jumbo*. New York: Viking, 1991.
This book recounts the facts of Jumbo's remarkable life with P. T. Barnum's menagerie in nineteenth-century London and America.

Wexo, John Bonnett. *Elephants*. San Diego, Calif.: Wildlife Education, Ltd., 1980.
Contains facts and photographs about elephants.

Wolkstein, Diane. *8,000 Stones*. Illustrated by Ed Young. Garden City, N.Y.: Doubleday, 1972.
This book received an honorable mention from the New York Academy of Sciences Children's Science Book Award.

Magazine Articles

"U.S. Bans Ivory Imports for Protection of the African Elephant." *Endangered Species Technical Bulletin* XIV, no. 6 (June 1989): 1-8. Department of the Interior, Washington, D.C.: U.S. Fish and Wildlife Service.
Articles on the banning of ivory to protect the elephant.

Tigers

THE TIGER

Hmong Traditional Tale

 any years ago, when the corn still came right up to the people's homes, there was a man named Plua Ndyua Nzeuh. He and his wife had three small children. Because they lived so far out in the forest, away from the homes of their families, the wife's younger sister, Yer, came to live with them and help take care of the children.

Plua Ndyua heard a gibbon chattering loudly in the forest and he went to see why all the animals were making such a fuss. He did not see the tiger who was under the tree the gibbon was in. After Plua Ndyua shot the gibbon with his gun, the gibbon fell out of the tree onto the ground. As Plua Ndyua was picking up the gibbon, the tiger pounced on him and ate him.

The tiger put on Plua Ndyua's clothes, picked up the gun, and held it to his shoulder. He slung the gibbon over his other shoulder. The tiger said, "Now I am a man."

He headed for Plua Ndyua's house. The sister Yer saw the tiger coming and said to the children's mother, "Here comes somebody. He is dressed like Plua Ndyua but he looks like a tiger."

The wife took a look and said, "Oh yes, that is Plua Ndyua all right."

Yer insisted that it did not look like Plua Ndyua to her. She called out, "You are not my brother-in-law."

The tiger replied as he got closer, "Oh yes, I am."

Plua Ndyua's wife had worked hard that day and was tired, so she gathered her three children and took them to bed. She bid goodnight to everyone and got ready to sleep.

Yer decided to hide upstairs that night. She fixed a bowl of hot red pepper, a bowl of salt, and a bowl of ashes from the fireplace. She took a blanket and climbed the ladder to the attic. She placed the three bowls on a shelf beside her on the storage platform.

During the night Yer heard crunching noises from downstairs. She was frightened and called down, "What are you eating that sounds like the sound of breaking bones?"

The tiger replied, "I am just chewing some stems of a hemp plant. Go to sleep, little sister."

Yer had trouble sleeping. Just as dawn was breaking the next morning, the tiger said, "Sister Yer, it is morning. Come down."

Yer was still worried so she answered, "No, I won't come down. I think I will stay up here."

"If you don't come down, I will come up," snarled the tiger and he started to climb up the ladder. Yer grabbed the bowl of salt and threw it into his eyes. The tiger screamed from the burning in his eyes. Then Yer threw a handful of the pepper at him and the tiger frantically started to rub his eyes with his forepaws. He fell to the floor and crawled to the door, saying "I am very thirsty, little sister. I am going down to the river for a drink."

When he got out of the house he ran to the river to wash his eyes. Yer heard him cry, "Oh, oh, oh!"

She quickly came down the ladder and gathered some food, got more red pepper, more salt, and more ashes. She went back up to the attic. Just as she put the pepper, salt, and ashes on the shelf, she heard the tiger return.

"I am back from the river. Are you coming down now or not?" he asked.

"I am not coming down," Yer told him.

"Then I am coming up," threatened the tiger and he started to climb up the ladder. Yer threw the bowl of hot pepper into his eyes, then the bowl of salt, and then the bowl of ashes. Again the tiger dropped to the floor, rubbing his eyes and writhing in pain. "Oh, oh, oh!" he moaned as he crawled to the door and ran to the river to wash his eyes.

A crow who often visited Yer flew to the top of the house. Yer told the bird to fly to her family. "Tell them a tiger ate my brother-in-law, my sister, and their children. Tell my family to come quickly."

"I will," squawked the crow, "but first give me some food and then I will take the message to your parents."

Yer gave the crow some food and after he ate it, he flew off toward her family's home. The crow flew directly to her father. "Yer sends word that a tiger has eaten all of the Plua Ndyua Nzeuh family. Only Yer is left. The tiger is trying to get her too and Yer begs you to come quickly."

All of Yer's family took their guns, spears, and sabers and hurried to save Yer. Yer was still fighting the tiger off with pepper, salt, and ashes. The tiger had made several more trips to the river. When Yer's family came, the tiger was at the river washing his swollen eyes again.

Yer told her family what had happened. Her oldest brother told her to call to the tiger and tell him she would become his wife. Yer shouted toward the river, "Tiger, tiger. My family is here. They want to talk with you. I will be your wife. My parents and my brothers and sisters have come to give me to you."

"Aha, that's good. I will be right there." As the tiger said this he hurried to the house. When the tiger saw how many people were there, he got quiet. Yer's brother began, "Oh brave one, let's talk."

While he was talking with the tiger, several of Yer's brothers went outside. They dug a hole in the path to the river and covered it over with some twigs and leaves. When they returned to the house, one of them said, "Dear tiger, your eyes look as if they hurt. Come to the river. Let us help you wash your poor eyes. We will help you."

"Poor future brother-in-law, your eyes are so swollen you must be having trouble seeing. Take an arm and the two of us will guide you to the river." The tiger walked between two of the brothers. Only the tiger walked on the path. When he came to the leaves covering the hole, he fell in.

Yer's brothers killed the tiger with their spears. Then Yer's family took her home with them.

► ● ◄

FOLKLORE

Tigers are native to Malaya, Sumatra, Assam, Bengal, and southern Asia. Tigers are known for being brave, man-killers, and shapeshifters, and have a reputation for viciousness, cruelty, and treachery. There is a Chinese version of the Red Riding Hood story in which a tiger, taking the place of the wolf in the European tales, eats the old woman.

The Hmong of southeast Asia believe that spirits can take the form of a tiger. During the three days after a body has been buried, its soul may be dragged into the jungle by evil spirits and there be transformed into a man-eating tiger. If such a tiger is shot, the evil spirits take the soul with them. In time it too turns into an evil spirit that causes harm. The Hmong say that if the track of a tiger shows five toes instead of the customary four, it is a magic soul-tiger. They also believe that a tiger can be a dead uncle who comes back in tiger form to take care of the family, orphans, etc.

When there is a killer tiger, some people believe they must try to catch the tiger alive, explain why it is necessary for them to kill it, and ask forgiveness for executing it.

Hill people of Bengal believe that if a man kills a tiger without divine orders, he or a near relative will in turn be killed by a tiger. Some people in the Malay peninsula believe that tigers live in houses and cities of their own. Tigers are also believed to be immortal. Others believe that eating tiger meat will give strength and courage to men. On the other hand, women should not eat the meat because it will make them too strong-minded. Charms are made from tiger whiskers. Koreans grind tiger bones into a powder and take it with wine for strength and sexual potency.

DISCUSSION

Description

The tiger (*Panthera tigris*) is the largest of all cats and is related to other members of the cat family, such as the lion, leopard, ocelot, lynx, jaguar, cheetah, mountain lion, puma, and panther, as well as the domestic cat. Subspecies of the tiger include the Indian tiger, Indochinese tiger, South Chinese tiger, Caspian tiger, Siberian tiger, Sumatran tiger, Javan tiger, and the Balinese tiger.

Tigers can weigh as much as 600 pounds (272 kilograms) and reach 11 feet (3.3 meters) in length. A tiger is a graceful, strong, and fierce animal. People who know both the tiger and the lion say that the tiger is more powerful.

The largest tigers live in southern Siberia and western China. The tigers of these colder regions grow thicker, rougher, and duller fur. Albinos, with faint brown stripes on white fur, have been found in northern China.

The stripes of the tiger are an excellent device for hiding in a forest with flickering shadows and faded marsh grass.

Behavior

Tigers are flesh-eating carnivores. In India their principal game foods are deer, wild pigs, antelope, and cattle. They also eat buffalo, but only the young or sick. Man-eating tigers are generally old tigers whose energy is failing and whose teeth are worn. Therefore, they find it easier to kill humans than wild prey.

Tigers usually hunt at night unless they are extremely hungry. At these times they will kill during the day. A tigress with young has to kill every five to six days to provide food. A tiger eats whatever it catches and they have been known to occasionally take rhino and elephant calves. Tigers have been known to swim from island to island searching for a better hunting ground, but they often go into the water on hot days just to cool off.

Although there are from two to six cubs in a litter, only rarely do more than two survive. The mother is affectionate and hunts food for the cubs when they can no longer live on her milk. She also teaches them to hunt and kill for themselves. After they have grown enough to master hunting skills, she leaves them.

A female tiger will have cubs only once in two or three years. If a tiger survives the first few months of life, it usually lives for about fifteen to twenty years.

Habitat

Tigers live in a varied environment including tropical rain forests, snow-covered coniferous and deciduous forests, mangrove swamps, and drier forest areas. Their source of food in the mangrove swamps at seaside are fish and even turtles. The home range for females is 8 square miles (20 square kilometers) while the range for males includes 23 to 40 square miles (60 to 100 square kilometers). Male ranges encompass those of several females. They maintain rights to home range by spraying urine on trees, bushes, and rocks along trails as well as scratching trees.

Historic Range

Tigers once ranged across Asia from the northern Middle East to Korea, from Siberia to the jungles of Java and Bali (see fig. 5.1). Reduced numbers indicate that the requirements for large prey and sufficient cover are becoming more difficult to meet. As big game animal herds dwindled, the tigers moved to new hunting grounds. Most areas that once had tiger populations have them no longer and tigers are either gone or seldom seen.

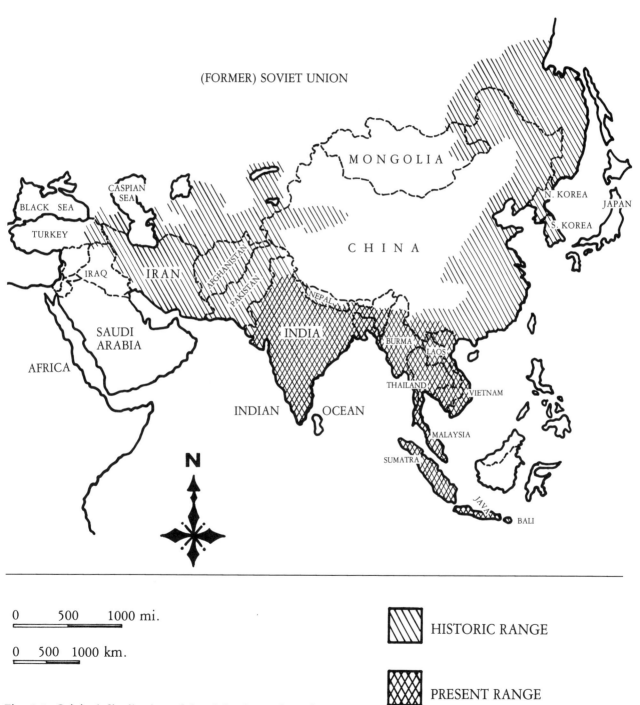

0   500   1000 mi.

0   500   1000 km.

HISTORIC RANGE

PRESENT RANGE

Fig. 5.1. Original distribution of the eight tiger subspecies.

Reasons for Endangerment and Attempts to Help

In the past fifty years, the world population of tigers has plummeted from over 100,000 individuals in eight subspecies to around 5,000 individuals in five subspecies. The Balinese tiger is extinct and the South Chinese and Caspian tigers are probably extinct. The last known Balinese tiger was a female shot at Sumbar Kima, West Bali, on September 27, 1937. All the surviving subspecies are endangered. Biologists say the remaining tiger populations are both too fragmented and too small for long-term survival. To prevent inbreeding, a reproducing population of tigers must number between 200 and 300 animals and this is a real problem.

The demise of the tigers is due to several reasons. A major problem is the destruction of habitat through deforestation and the destruction of wild game on which tigers feed. Agricultural encroachment has created a problem in which tigers subsist in part or wholly on domestic cattle and buffalo for their chief source of food. The tiger is also sought for its fur and as a trophy. Before the world realized the near-extinction of these animals was close, their fur was prized for fashion's sake. It was used in coats, decorations, and hats. Folkloric beliefs also contributed to the tiger's demise, as people believed that eating tiger meat gave strength and courage, and that ground bones taken with wine gave strength and sexual potency to the ingester. Their whiskers were also made into charms. Many captive tigers are trained to perform in circus acts.

Things are changing for the tiger though. There are worldwide efforts to amass funds to support tiger conservation. For instance, a dozen reserves have been established in India, which has helped somewhat. Tigers are protected by law in Sumatra. Conflicts between tigers and people can be reduced through environmental planning and forest conservation practices and by teaching people how to avoid confrontation with the big cats. The price tag to accomplish this is high.

Ironically, the tiger population in Vietnam may have actually increased as a result of the strife. The tiger diet is augmented by fallen victims of war.

More than 1,000 Siberian tigers are kept in zoos around the world providing a gene pool that could assure the survival of the species. Modern zoos are devoting efforts to captive breeding. Management includes animal exchanges between zoos to assure successful propagation.

TIGER ACTIVITIES

Tigers and Literature

• Read the tiger story at the beginning of this chapter. Yer was resourceful in fighting the tiger. What would you do if you were in a similar situation? List some other ways to avoid being killed by the tiger.

• Ask your librarian to help you find any local legends about tigers or panthers. Most areas have old panther stories that are either tall tales or legends. Select one to tell to the class, when you are camping, or when you spend a night at a friend's.

Tigers as Symbols

• Tigers are used in advertisements to sell gasoline and cars. What characteristics of the tiger lend themselves to such portrayals? What other products benefit from association with members of the cat family? Create an artistic representation of these commercial applications, such as a diorama, mobile, or dramatization.

Tigers and the Environment

- One of the scientist's most valuable tools is observation. The scientist uses observation to investigate facts and develop hypotheses. Arrange to spend half an hour at the zoo observing any of the following cats: tiger, lion, leopard, ocelot, lynx, jaguar, cheetah, mountain lion, puma, or panther. Then spend half an hour observing a common house cat. Record their behaviors, comparing their differences and similarities.

- In some regions of India, great problems have arisen as human uses encroach upon areas that have always been tiger habitats. In many cases, the tigers have abandoned their traditional prey and become man-eaters. Research this conflict and discuss possible compromises, including those now being tested by the Indian authorities.

- A similar situation has occurred in Colorado's mountain regions, as human occupation stretches into areas inhabited by mountain lions. See the accompanying articles from the *Rocky Mountain News*, which contain information as well as the story of a young man's death from a mountain lion attack (see fig. 5.2, pages 62-63, "Homes Encroach on Lions' Habitat"). Read the article "Put Fear into Pumas, Official Says" (see fig. 5.2, pages 62-63) and make lists of what you should and should not do if you run across a mountain lion in the wild.

(Text continues on page 64.)

Humans, cougars collide in foothills

Homes Encroach on Lions' Habitat

By Gary Gerhardt

Rocky Mountain News Staff Writer

On the afternoon Scott Lancaster was found dead from a mountain lion attack in Idaho Springs, state wildlife officer Jerry Apker entered Clear Creek Secondary School and came face-to-face with a young girl, tears steaming down her face.

"She saw my uniform and looked me in the eye, asking, 'Why?'

"I stood with a handful of brochures on how to guard against lion attacks and was at a complete loss to explain it," Apker said.

Lancaster, 18, was attacked on Jan. 14 as he jogged on a rocky hillside above his Idaho Springs high school.

Wildlife officials theorize the running may have triggered a "cat-and-mouse" response in the 3-year-old male cougar, which attacked from behind, apparently killing the young man before he could attempt to defend himself.

The lion, still in the area when the body was found, was shot and killed. An examination indicated it suffered neither from rabies nor physical injuries.

Lancaster is believed to be the first human ever killed by a lion in Colorado, and his death sent a shock wave through the Front Range, where encounters between humans and cougars have been on the rise in the last six years.

In recent days, there has been a spate of lion incidents, including 17 sightings last month in the Boulder area alone.

In the weeks since the attack, officials from the Colorado Division of Wildlife and Boulder parks have spent countless hours addressing the concerns of people who live and play in the foothills.

"Even some who have lived here a long time now believe the lions have gone mad," said Mike Sanders of Boulder County Parks and Open Spaces.

Sanders added that it doesn't help to explain that an attack by a mountain lion, cougar, puma—all synonyms for the same animal—is about as common as being struck by lightning. Nor does it help to tell someone who is frightened that one of the things that makes Colorado beautiful and desirable is that it still contains wild places and wild creatures.

"They just want to be safe," he said. "Some people are so afraid they want the lions eliminated."

But what appears to be a much larger group of people is not only willing to accept the dangers of living in lion country but also opposes any attempt to remove or constrain the animals, citing both environmental and ethical reasons.

"A guy near Nederland shot a lion last week after it got into a chicken coop, and many people have called saying they think he overreacted and we should have strict laws governing when a lion can be shot," Sanders said.

Because fatal attacks by cougars on humans are so rare, the most repeated question is what went wrong in Idaho Springs?

But the most likely answer is that nothing went wrong, that such attacks have happened in the past and can be expected to happen again, as the suburbs reach deeper into the lions' habitat.

Over the past 100 years, there have been 54 documented attacks by cougars on humans in the U.S. and Canada. Eleven of those attacks resulted in fatalities. All but two of those deaths (including Lancaster's) were children under 16.

In earlier times, cougar attacks and kills were probably more common.

In *The Puma: Legendary Lion of the Americas*, Jim Bob Tinsley

Put Fear into Pumas, Official Says

Colorado wildlife officials say an aggressive posture may be the best way for people to handle confrontations with cougars along the Front Range.

Area wildlife manager Jerry Apker of the Colorado Division of Wildlife said such an approach may put fear of humans into lions now used to being around people.

"If you simply encounter a lion—that is, see it at some distance—we still recommend you avoid eye contact that the cat might perceive as a threat, speak quietly and back slowly away," Apker said.

"But if it appears an actual confrontation is about to take place, we believe you should make immediate and threatening eye contact with the lion while making yourself look as large as possible. You can pull your jacket sides out, stand as tall as possible, anything to make yourself look more formidable."

At the same time, shout, make lots of noise and look around for rocks that can be thrown or a large stick that can be used to beat on the ground or as a defensive weapon if necessary.

"A couple of things remain constant," he said. "Above all, never turn and run. This almost always triggers the prey-predator response, and the cat will attack.

"If it does, don't drop to the ground and assume a fetal position (as) in a bear attack. The

Fig. 5.2. *Rocky Mountain News* (February 3, 1991): **10, 29**. Reprinted with permission of the *Rocky Mountain News*.

Fig. 5.2. — (*Continued*)

Residents Must Learn to Live with Risk

COUGARS from 62

recounts some of these attacks and offers a photograph of the tombstone of Philip Tanner in Lewisville, Pa., a millwright killed by a puma on May 6, 1751. On Tanner's headstone is carved the figure of a cougar.

In recent years, wildlife officials suspect children, for a variety of reasons, have been the primary target of lion attacks.

First and most obviously, children are small. Aside from their main prey — deer — lions eat raccoons, rabbits, rodents, beaver, porcupine, coyote, marten, skunk and, if available, domestic livestock. In other words, they are accustomed to hunting smaller mammals.

Also, when out of doors, children often move at one speed — wide open — which triggers lions' prey-predator chase response. Children also have a tendency to squeal when they run, which to a lion's ear may sound, like the distress call of a small animal.

No one knows exactly how many of the state's estimated 1,500-3,000 lions live on the Front Range.

Division of wildlife biologist Kathi Green says models based on known sizes of home ranges for lions are the only barometer for making an educated guess.

"We figure, given that female lions need 10 to 40 square miles of home range, there could be 35 to 50 lions in the Boulder County areas," she said.

But the model is questionable because research on lion home ranges has been in remote, wild areas where prey bases are far smaller than they are along the Front Range.

As people have moved into the foothills, deer populations have exploded, thanks to bans on hunting near populated areas. And homeowners often grow lawns, gardens and shrubs, which attract the deer, which in turn attract the lions.

So if more people means more deer, which in turn means more lions, does that imply that there must be more danger as well?

Sanders said he does not believe that has to be the equation.

The simplest answer might be to move the lions. But there are practical, environmental, biological and ethical reasons not to choose that solution.

First, although lions are relatively easy to catch in leghold traps and snares, after capture they often go into a rage, injuring themselves so severely that they have to be destroyed.

And even if a number of lions were removed, with deer populations so high other lions would soon move in to take their places.

Another suggestion is to cull the deer herds. But hunting, the method the wildlife division most often emnploys, is not an option in populated areas.

Perhaps the most compelling argument against removing the deer, Apker said, is that it could backfire. Depriving lions of their primary food source would only encourage them to turn elsewhere: domestic pets, livestock and possibly humans.

A better answer, according to division of wildlife director Perry Olson, is for people to learn how to coexist with a hazard that is, after all, largely of their own making.

"People learn to adapt and live around rattlesnakes," he said. "It's a real, real tragedy when someone gets killed," Olson added, "but if we want open spaces and to live around wild creatures, there are risks involved."

PUMAS from 62

worst thing you can do is lose your footing."

Unlike canines, felines not only bite, but have four paws full of razor-sharp claws. They often grab an animal with their front claws and use the rear claws to disembowel it.

As for non-lethal weapons that may be carried in the field, Apker said he's looking into the use of Pepper Mace and perhaps riot-control tear gas that might be carried by humans in lion country.

"We haven't had a chance yet to test a lot of these products, but there couldn't be a better time than now to do it," he said.

— *Gary Gerhardt*

- Create a board game. Using the sources listed in the resource bibliography (see pages 67-68), create playing cards about tigers or cougars. The board should emphasize the environment and might include free spaces, go-back spaces, advance spaces, and a safe space. Try out your game and refine it.

- Using the article "Three Orphaned Lion Cubs Trapped" (see fig. 5.3), make a list of things you think people will do to rehabilitate these cubs. Research the techniques rehabilitators use to prepare animals for reentry to the wild. Write to the Division of Wildlife requesting information on retraining animals for the wild or for a speaker to visit your class. Would these techniques be useful for villages in India that have problems with tigers?

Three orphaned lion cubs trapped

By Michael Romano
Rocky Mountain News Staff Writer

NEDERLAND — A search in rugged canyonland this weekend bagged a prized catch: three of the four lion cubs orphaned when their mother was shot to death late last month.

Until they were snagged in injury-free traps, the cubs had wandered for weeks through the steep terrain of Boulder Canyon, foraging on carcasses or snatching food from homeowners.

One of the cougar cubs was seen licking the dried fat off a barbecue grill.

The cubs, about 3 months old and weighing 15 to 20 pounds, were transported yesterday to the home of a private animal "rehabilitator" in Wetmore, a community in the foothills near Pueblo. They eventually will be returned to the wild.

"They've ranged quite a distance from the point where their mother was shot — a mile or so," said Bob Farentinos, an animal ecologist who helped coordinate the search and successfully baited the traps with dog and cat food.

The mother of the four cubs was killed Jan. 25 by a Nederland homeowner who discovered the 90-pound lion outside a chicken coop. One of the four cubs was killed Thursday, struck by a car on a highway in Boulder Canyon.

Lion cubs generally remain with the mother for about 14 months. The cubs probably will be released in southern Colorado.

Cece Sanders, a rehabilitator who has done similar work for the state division of wildlife, will keep the cubs in a large cage for up to a year, giving them time to grow and learn to hunt.

In the absence of complicating factors such as disease, the three cubs should have a good chance at survival after rehabilitation, said Kathi Green, a wildlife biologist with the central region of the Colorado Division of Wildlife.

"The main thing is to keep them away from humans," said Green.

"And there are lots of techniques rehabilitators use so that animals get fed without coming in contact with humans."

The lion cubs, who have sharp claws and fairly large baby teeth, were trapped without injury late Saturday and early yesterday.

They were captured in an area about 4 miles east of Nederland on the north side of Boulder Canyon, in the back yard of the home with the barbecue grill.

Farentinos said he and state wildlife officials monitored the meandering cats with the help of residents' sightings.

The search grew more intense because wildlife officials feared that the animals would start associating humans with food. Under those circumstances, the animals would either have been destroyed or placed in zoos.

"You'd have a situation where they could be dangerous because they'd be totally unafraid of humans," said Farentinos.

Fig. 5.3. *Rocky Mountain News* (February 18, 1991): 7. Reprinted with permission of the *Rocky Mountain News*.

- Read the newspaper article (see fig. 5.4) on "Lions' Strength, Agility Awesome, Expert Says." Using the facts from this article, write an adventure story about someone encountering a mountain lion. From your knowledge of and research on tigers, make a list of changes that would have to be made to your story, to make it realistic, if the person were to encounter a tiger.

Lions' strength, agility awesome, expert says

By Gary Gerhardt
Rocky Mountain News Staff Writer

Cougars have a reputation for ferocity and cowardice, and while capable of showing either characteristic, there's no way to judge their mood when the wrong time comes.

"Even in the same litter, one cub will be overly aggressive, the other almost shy. But you just never can take any of them for granted," says Allen Anderson.

Anderson is a Colorado Division of Wildlife researcher who spent most of the 1980s in the canyons of western Colorado trapping, radio-collaring and tracking cougars.

"The dogs would run one up a tree and it would just raise the roof, growling and howling and thrashing about," he said.

"Run another up, and it about goes to sleep waiting for you to fix the tranqualizer."

It's this unpredictability of these large, mysterious cats that is most unnerving when they are unexpectedly encountered.

"One thing people who live around lions should know is how truly powerful they are," Anderson said.

"To kill a deer, they jump on its back, sink their claws in and bite through the back of the neck and sever the spine.

"We found one elk a lion killed by leaping onto its back, reaching around to hook the head and jerked it back so hard the animal broke its neck."

Anderson said lions don't look as formidable as they are because they have such small heads.

"But you peel back the hide on a scale and in males there's a crest an inch high that the jaw muscles attach to, giving them awesome jaw power," he said.

Anderson said he once tranqualized a cougar to put a radio collar on, but it came out of the stupor for a couple of moments and started after the dogs.

"One of the men with me weighed more than 200 pounds and the other fellow was 180," Anderson said. "They both grabbed the cat's tail and it dragged them through deep snow for quite a few feet before the drug took over and it dropped."

Giving some idea of the cougar's leaping ability, Anderson said his crew once treed a young cat that jumped and landed 30 feet from the tree.

Like house cats, cougars are extremely curious, Anderson said.

"We had a collar on one cat and were flying over an isolated stretch when we spotted a pickup some hunter had parked and walked away from," he said.

"From the radio signal, that cat must have been in the truck."

Once, he said, his crew was trying to find one collared animal and when they got within half a mile, the signal started growing fainter meaning the animal was running away.

"But as soon as we stopped, it stopped. And when we just waited, pretty soon it started back looking for us," Anderson said.

In working with 47 lions, Anderson said he never had any problems.

"But there have been a few we cornered that looked like it would be a good idea to stay away from them — so we did," he said.

Fig. 5.4. *Rocky Mountain News* (February 3, 1991): 28. Reprinted with permission of the *Rocky Mountain News*.

- After reading the newspaper article "Lion Shot after Dining on Chickens and Geese" (see fig. 5.5) and the other articles in this chapter, make lists for:

1. What do mountain lions like to eat? How are these foods similar to or different from those in a tiger's diet?

2. What are some of the reasons for more encounters between mountain lions and people? Which of these factors might also be responsible for human-tiger conflict?

3. What are some possible solutions to this dilemma?

Lion shot after dining on chickens and geese

By Kevin McCullen
Rocky Mountain News Boulder Bureau

BOULDER — A Nederland-area man shot and killed a mountain lion after it rampaged through a chicken house next to a home, authorities said yesterday.

Officers from the Colorado Division of Wildlife were planning to retrieve the carcass of the cat, which appeared to be a female weighing about 90 pounds, said division spokesman Todd Malmsbury.

Boulder County resident Marvin Dewey was visiting a home Friday night when he saw a mountain lion standing near a hutch for chickens and geese. The animal remained stationary when Dewey approached, and he returned to his pickup for a gun.

Dewey fired once at the lion with a .357-caliber Magnum, killing it, Malmsbury said.

Dewey was not available for comment. Malmsbury said the shooting appeared to be within legal guidelines, which permit someone to kill a lion if it is threatening them or attacking livestock.

"The lion made short work of the chickens and geese," Malmsbury said.

It was the third lion killed this month after encounters with humans or domestic animals. Last week, a mountain lion was shot in Colorado Springs after it killed a cocker spaniel outside a home. A high school student jogging outside Idaho Springs was killed by a mountain lion two weeks ago, and the animal was later killed.

Lions also have been seen recently in the Pinebrook Hills area outside Boulder and near Nederland, Malmsbury said. Along the Front Range, lion encounters are becoming more numerous as homes are built farther into their mountain habitat.

"We want to emphasize that people's actions usually lead to consequences with animals," he said.

Increases in the deer population also are responsible in part for more lion sightings, since deer are a principal food of the big cats, Malmsbury said.

Fig. 5.5. *Rocky Mountain News* (January 29, 1991). Reprinted with permission of the *Rocky Mountain News*.

RESOURCE BIBLIOGRAPHY

Books

Clutton-Brock, Juliet. *Eyewitness Books: Cat*. New York: Knopf, 1991.
The anatomy, behavior, habitats, and other aspects of wild and domestic cats are presented in text and photographs.

Complete Field Guide to American Wildlife. Assembled by Jay Ellis Ransom. New York: Harper & Row, 1981.
Information on wildlife habits and habitats complete with maps.

Cowcher, Helen. *Tigress*. New York: Farrar, Straus & Giroux, 1991.
A dramatic story of conservation. The tigress is out hunting for food and the sanctuary ranger devises a plan to save both predator and prey.

George, Jean Craighead. *The Moon of the Mountain Lions*. Illustrated by Ron Parker. New York: HarperCollins, 1991.
The story of a young mountain lion in Washington state during the month of August. Migration and mating matter.

Holmes, Martha. *Deadly Animals*. Illustrated by Mike Vaughan. New York: Atheneum, 1991.
Holmes gives the young reader a chilling look at eleven of nature's deadliest creations. The accompanying artwork is dramatic and powerful.

Larrick, Nancy. *Cats Are Cats*. Illustrated by Ed Young. New York: Philomel, 1988.
A compilation of forty-two poems exploring the world of cats. The artwork is rich and appealing.

Lewis, Sharon. *Tiger!* Illustrated by Linda Roberts. New York: Harper & Row, 1990.
Tiger! gives information on tigers and includes a punch-out hat for the reader to wear. The accompanying art is cut-paper technique.

Liptak, Karen. *Out in the Night*. Illustrated by Sandy Ferguson Fuller. Tucson, Ariz.: Harbinger House, 1989.
Everyone knows that there are "things that go bump in the night." The descriptive text covers many things that hoot, howl, bellow, and snort at night. The artwork details the habits and habitat of nocturnal animals in fourteen locations around the world.

Livo, Norma J., and Dia Cha. *Folk Stories of the Hmong*. Englewood, Colo.: Libraries Unlimited, 1991.
This compilation of folk stories contains several with tiger characters. There is an introduction to the history and background of the Hmong people as well as photographs and samples of their stitchery folk art.

Martin, Louise. *Tigers*. Vero Beach, Fla.: Rourke Publishers, 1988.
Martin describes the remaining species of tigers, how their survival is threatened, and efforts to protect them.

Royston, Angela. *Eye Openers Jungle Animals*. Photography by Philip Dowell. New York: Aladdin Books, 1991.
> Simple text and detailed illustrations introduce youngsters to creatures of the wild from around the world.

Tigers of the World: The Biology, Biopolitics, Management, and Conservation of an Endangered Species. Park Ridge, N.J.: Noyes Publications, 1986.
> This book is a collection of forty-six papers presented at an international symposium sponsored by the Minneapolis Zoological Garden and the IUCN/SSC Captive Breeding and Cat Specialist Groups. It covers all facets of tiger biology and plots out a global tiger conservation plan. It should be useful to anyone interested in conservation strategies for any large species.

Book and Tape

Weir, Bob, and Wendy Weir. *Panther Dream: A Story of the African Rainforest*. New York: Huperion, 1991.

_____. *Panther Dream and Panther Dance*. Tape. New York: Midnite Kitty, 1991. No. 56282-0.
> *Panther Dream* is the story of a young boy who encounters a panther that teaches him how to conserve life. (The book and tape is a set.)

Bob Weir, guitarist and singer for the Grateful Dead, and his sister Wendy will use the proceeds from this book and tape to fund rain forest reforestation and educational projects in Africa.

Leopards

THE MONKEY AND THE LEOPARD

An African Folktale

 ne day Leopard went off on a hunting trip, as he so often did. He was very hungry because he had not had anything to eat for several nights. He walked softly, almost silently, through the jungle with his eyes glowing and his tongue hanging out and slobbering with the thought of the food he would soon get. His tail swished this way and that as he walked. Suddenly, he fell into a trap, a pit that had been covered with limbs and leaves. Leopard was scared silly with his predicament and raced from one side of the pit to the other. He jumped as high as he could up the sides of the walls, but all to no avail. He was trapped! What should he now do?

He thought, "If I cry out, the hunter will no doubt hear me and he will come and kill me. If I don't cry out, I'll die from hunger since I'm very hungry already. But maybe if I cry out some other animal will hear me and set me free. What do I have to lose by crying out?"

So Leopard roared a panic-stricken roar and, sure enough, the animals came to see who was caught in the trap. But as soon as the animals, one by one, saw that it was Leopard in the pit, they hurried off without offering to help at all. Leopard was in no better situation than before.

Leopard yelled, "Please help me, brother gazelle. Help me out, brother impala."

But the animals shook their heads. "Help Leopard? I don't think so! We have problems of our own and those problems would be greater if Leopard were out of the pit. Who can approach Leopard without putting his own life in danger?" And so they hurried on down the path, leaving Leopard in his desperate plight.

Meanwhile, the little white-nosed monkey heard all the commotion from his perch on the umbrella tree, where he spent most of every day watching the comings and goings of the jungle. He was pulling fruit off the tree and having a great time eating it when he became just too curious to know who was caught in the trap. He swung down from the tree and cautiously approached the edge of the pit. As he did so, the roaring turned to whining. Monkey could not keep himself from going right up to the edge of the pit. He leaned over, looked in, and saw Leopard all dirty from trying to free himself and all tired out from his effort.

"Oh, Leopard," called the little monkey clown, "what are you doing down there in that pit? Can't you get out?"

"Praise to Allah," replied Leopard with a great relief in his voice, "you've come, Monkey. Have mercy on me in this deep pit and help me out."

Monkey thought about it. He knew all about Leopard. He knew that Leopard ate just about every living thing in the jungle, including monkeys, and he was more than a little suspicious, knowing as he did Leopard's character.

"If I pulled you up, wouldn't you be likely to eat me?" asked Monkey.

"Oh, Monkey. You misjudge me greatly. I would not eat such a kind benefactor. You have my word on it."

Monkey was still not convinced. "Let's get this straight. If I pull you up, you will not eat me?"

"By my ancestors, I swear it," promised Leopard. "I would not do such a thing. Do not be afraid. Please rescue me."

Monkey was still not convinced. "How do I know you're not just saying this because you are about to die? Animals in the jungle know Leopard and know what your eating habits are. Have you ever spared another animal's life?"

Leopard began to plead, saying that he was misunderstood, that he would change his ways and become a model citizen of the jungle if only Monkey would help him out of what would soon become his grave.

"I don't know," said Monkey, "that I'd be doing the right thing for myself and the other animals of the jungle."

Leopard cried and moaned at this rebuff and said, "Monkey, if you help me out I'll be your friend for life and a friend to all your cousins."

Monkey was naturally soft-hearted, so he gave in, saying, "Leopard, you have pledged your word on your ancestors. We shall see. I'll help you out of the pit."

With those words, Monkey let his long tail down into the pit where Leopard could catch it. With great effort, Monkey pulled Leopard out of the hole. Monkey was still trying to catch his breath and was about to strike up a conversation when he noticed a familiar gleam in Leopard's eyes. Leopard's attitude had changed very suddenly and Monkey knew he was in mortal danger. Monkey began to shake with fear and fright as he asked, "Leopard, are you going to go back on your sacred oath? Are you going to eat me, without whom you surely would have died?"

"Monkey, don't you know the law of the jungle?" asked Leopard. "I will still surely die unless I get something to eat and there you stand, all fat and sassy. You decided to help me. Help me further by allowing me to eat you."

It dawned on Monkey that he was practically doomed, but still he tried to think up some way to escape. He tried to reason with Leopard and then to appeal to Leopard's sense of fair play, but all seemed lost. The animals filed past the pit one by one and as each passed by, Monkey explained the situation: how he had saved Leopard; how Leopard had promised not to eat him, even invoking a sacred oath; and how Monkey himself was now about to die. He tried to get each one of the animals to condemn Leopard, but no one did. Every animal was deathly afraid of going against Leopard and they urged Monkey to give in and allow himself to be eaten so that all the other animals could escape.

Leopard became impatient and had just decided to end all the conversation and the stalling by Monkey when a tortoise walked by, carrying, as always, the burden of his heavy shell.

"Oh, Tortoise, my good friend," began Monkey, "something very sad is happening to me. I rescued Leopard from certain death. He promised not to harm me and now he is soon to make my death certain. I changed from benefactor to prey in his eyes and you can see how his eyes glare at me now. Please give us a verdict in this case! If you find that I am in the wrong, I will allow myself to be eaten."

Tortoise was quite intrigued by the situation, but could not believe that Monkey had found the strength to pull Leopard out of the deep pit.

Monkey furrowed his brow. "I do not lie, Tortoise. Ask Leopard. He will tell you that it is so."

Leopard confirmed the details but added, "That is not the point. The point is that I am hungry and I have nothing else to eat besides Monkey here."

"You are certainly correct there," nodded the turtle, "but when I investigate a case I do not like to go on hearsay. I need actual evidence. All the elements are here to reenact this dreadful event—Monkey, pit, Leopard, and me. Can you show me, Leopard, how it happened that you fell into the pit?"

"If I show you, Tortoise, I am afraid Monkey will run away," Leopard suggested.

"Ah, but brother Leopard," reassured Tortoise, "I will be here to guard him. He will not run away."

With this reassurance, Leopard jumped into the pit with a single bound.

Tortoise turned to Monkey. "Don't you know, Monkey, that if you play with fire you will surely get burned? That if you flirt with danger, someday danger will overtake you?"

Monkey said, "Leopard cannot change his spots. He is what he is and I still can't regret having tried to help someone." And with that he ran off and quickly leaped into an umbrella tree. After he had swung up to the very top, he turned back and saw Tortoise staring into the pit and saying to Leopard, "Stay there in peace, brother Leopard, and never forget this: our character makes us what we are. It can save us or it can destroy us."

►●◄

FOLKLORE

The leopard is a predator feared by man and beast. Its reputation is one of stealth and cunning. The Bible uses the figure of the leopard as a symbol of savagery, on a par with lions and wolves. As an example, the fate of transgressors is given in a verse in the Old Testament:

> Wherefore a lion out of the forest shall slay them, and a wolf of the evenings shall spoil them, a leopard shall watch over their cities: every one that goeth out thence shall be torn in pieces: because their transgressions are many, and their backslidings are increased.
>
> —Jeremiah 5:6

The saying, "A leopard cannot change its spots," is used to illustrate that people, as well as animals, cannot be expected to change their ways. The story of the monkey and the leopard at the beginning of this chapter helps make this point.

Rudyard Kipling, in his delightful collection of children's tales, *Just So Stories*, discusses how the leopard got its spots in the first place. Kipling's words need to be read aloud but to paraphrase this story, the leopard lived in the "seclusively bare, hot, shining High Veldt" where his colors matched the environment perfectly. Thus hidden, leopard could surprise intended prey "out of their jumpsome lives."

The story goes on to tell of how the leopard and its hunting partner, the Ethiopian, were highly successful hunters until the game moved away to an area where they blended perfectly with the environment. "Baviaan, the dog-headed, barking Baboon, who is Quite the Wisest Animal in All of South Africa" suggested that the leopard and the Ethiopian move to where their game had migrated. On arriving, the hunting pair found that their intended prey blended perfectly with their surroundings, while they, the predators, stood out like "ripe bananas in a smoke house." First, the Ethiopian changed his skin so that he blended into the new environment. Next, the Ethiopian persuaded the leopard to change its skin. The leopard debated over whether to have stripes like the zebra or spots like the giraffe. It decided on spots, but did not want them "too vulgar-big" like the giraffe's, so it opted for clusters of small spots, which the Ethiopian applied with the leftover black from his hands. The Ethiopian touched the leopard with all five fingers of the hand, leaving clusters of five little black dots—some of which smeared when his hand slipped—all over the body of the leopard.

When the boy felt he was old enough and needed to make a sacrifice, as his mother had suggested, the leopard went to the marketplace, scared all the people away, and brought the boy the snails, kola nuts, and palm nuts he needed. The leopard also brought fine clothes for the boy to wear.

When the boy thought it was time to marry, the leopard helped him win the hand of the king's daughter with an ingenious plan. The leopard killed the princess after giving the boy the secret for bringing her back to life. The king gave his daughter in marriage to the boy who had restored her.

The leopard and the boy continued their lifelong friendship even after the boy's marriage, until his wife discovered their secret. She told her father, who had the leopard killed. A tortoise reminded the boy of the secret he had used to revive the princess, so he used it to bring the leopard back to life. The tortoise, however, suggested that such a friendship between a man and a leopard was not natural in either the human world or the animal world and suggested that they part ways. The two fast friends did part company and to this day there is no great friendship between humans and leopards.

DISCUSSION

Description

The leopard is one of the largest members of the cat family. A large male may weigh more than 200 pounds (90 kilograms), stand 28 inches (70 centimeters) tall at the shoulders, and be 5 feet (1.5 meters) long, not including a tail of 35 inches (90 centimeters). The leopard was formerly known as *pard* or *pardus* and is also called *panther* (*Panthera pardus*). The name *leopard* was originally given to the cat we now call *cheetah*. A leopard's color can vary from a pale yellowish gray to a yellowish red, with whitish underparts. Spots are present over the entire body, but on the back and sides they are formed into rosettes or circles. Woodland leopards are generally smaller than those of the open country, as their smaller size makes them more maneuverable in the woods. Woodland leopards also have darker spots than open-field leopards. This particular coloration helps them to hide among the shadows of the woods.

Behavior

Leopards are chiefly crepuscular (hunting at twilight) or nocturnal hunters, although they will occasionally be found basking in the sun. They are solitary as a rule, but a male and female may hunt in pairs during and after the mating season. The male remains close for three months or so after the birth of young to aid in their care and protection. There is no definite breeding season. The female produces a litter of two to four cubs, usually three, after a gestation period of three months.

Leopard calls range from coughs to growls to deep purring sounds. Leopards are good swimmers and, pound-for-pound, the strongest of the felines. They can carry prey equal to their own weight high into a tree.

Leopards eat any animal they can catch but generally prey on small and medium-sized antelopes or deer. They seem to particularly enjoy the taste of dogs and, in Africa, monkeys and baboons. Leopards are very fast and can attain speeds of 35 miles (60 kilometers) per hour, but lack the endurance to run down fast or elusive prey. They normally hunt by stealth, either lying in wait or actively stalking prey until close enough to catch it with a short burst of speed. Large prey animals are killed with a bite to the neck or by strangulation after the leopard closes its jaws on the windpipe. After making a kill, the leopard removes the victim's stomach and internal organs, which it may bury. Only then does it start feeding on the carcass. If the prey is too large to be eaten in one sitting, the leopard carries the remains to the high branches of a tree. Leopards have discovered that domestic livestock is the easiest prey and, because of this, have increasingly become at odds with people. Leopards have been known to eat humans and a single leopard was reported to have killed more than 100.

Habitat

Leopards are quite versatile and adaptable, occupying habitats ranging from dry grasslands to jungles. They have the greatest geographical distribution of any wildcat, being found over most of Africa south of the Sahara and from the Middle East and India north into central Asia and south into the East Indies.

Panthera pardus is endangered throughout its range (Africa, Asia Minor, India, Southeast Asia, China, Malasia, and Indonesia). It is threatened in east and central Africa, however. *Neofelis nebulosa*, the "clouded leopard," is endangered throughout its range (Southeast and south central Asia and Taiwan). *Panthera uncia*, the "snow leopard," is endangered throughout its central Asia range. *Felis bengalensis bengalensis* is endangered throughout its range in eastern Asia.

Historic Range and Current Distribution

The leopard, being quite adaptable, originally ranged over most of Africa and Asia. It is now rare in Asia, North Africa, and west Africa, but relatively plentiful in East and Central Africa (see fig. 6.1).

Reasons for Decline and Attempts to Help

The leopard seems more adaptable to the presence and activities of humans than do many threatened species and has a fairly large range. It is, however, confronted by a familiar set of problems: persecution as a predator, value as a trophy, commercial appeal of its gorgeous fur, and loss of habitat. The wider establishment of agriculture has caused scarcity of natural prey and has caused increased conflict between the cats and humans. Leopard pelts have been in demand since biblical times, but the 1960s brought a substantial increase in the demand for the furs of spotted cats. Poaching became widespread and many leopard populations were decimated. In the 1960s, as many as 50,000 leopard skins were marketed annually, of which nearly 10,000 were imported to the United States.[1]

National laws and international agreements have stemmed this demand and reduced the fur traffic. Nevertheless, only rigid enforcement of game laws can help some species of leopard survive.

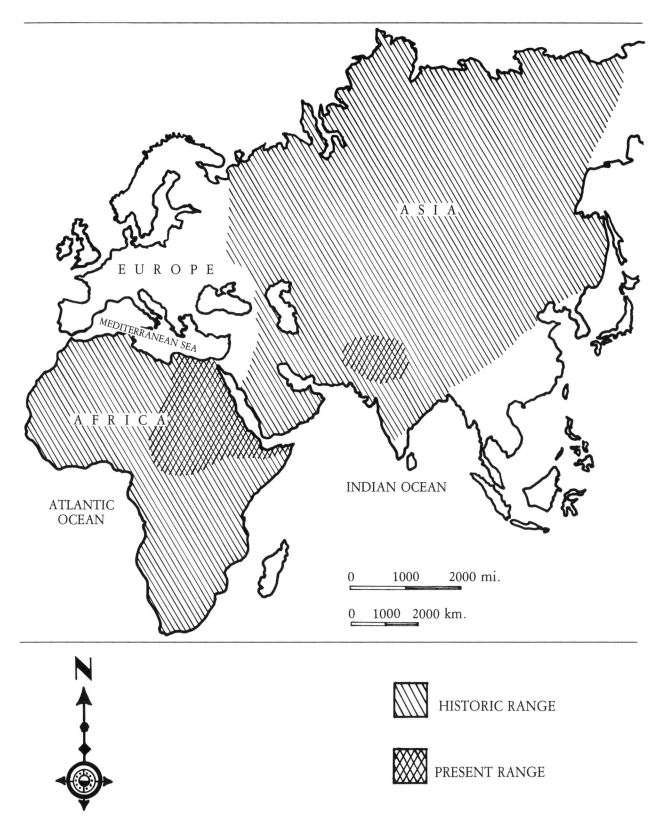

Fig. 6.1. Present and historic range of the leopard.

LEOPARD ACTIVITIES

Leopards and the Environment

- Records exist of a single leopard killing more than 100 humans. The so-called Rudraprayag man-eater is credited with killing 125 humans between 1918 and 1926. Research the effects of leopards on humans, starting with Corbett's book, *Man-Eaters of India*, listed in the bibliography of this chapter.

- The leopard has a keen sense of sight, but its hearing is not the best. List ways this might be detrimental to the leopard and useful to others in its environment.

Leopards and Characteristics of the Cat Family

- Joy Adamson deciphered some of the communication signals of the leopard, Penny, whom she raised from a one-month-old cub. Compare these signals to those of your cat, if you have one.

      Eyes half closed = danger

      Dilated pupils = excitement

      Flattened ears = danger (threat)

      Tail twitching = danger (threat)

- Joy Adamson raised, at different times, lions (Elsa is the most famous one), a cheetah named Pippa, and a leopard named Penny. Adamson observed that leopards were harder to understand than the other two species and were less reliable; that is, she never felt that she could fully relax around Penny. How would you account for this difference within the same general family of felines? Are some breeds of domestic cats better around people than others? Which breeds are the easiest to be around? Which are the most difficult?

- Joy Adamson's books on animals were written from her very detailed observations of these animals. Keep a diary for three weeks, making detailed observations about your pet. If you have two pets, such as a dog and a cat, compare the characteristics of each. Bring the information to class and compare with your classmates' results.

Leopards as an Endangered Species

- The leopard, particularly the *Felis bengalensis bengalensis*, is an endangered animal. Make a list of the problems that led to its near-extinction. What conservation plans are being used to help leopards survive?

Leopards and the Arts

• Reenact the folktale of the Ethiopian giving the leopard its spots.

• Produce a readers' theatre script in which the leopard is given its spots. Use the Kipling tale referred to in this chapter or write your own retelling.

• Make a "leopard skin" by dipping your fingers in black tempera paint and marking on a yellow cloth.

• Study the environment that is favorable for the leopard. Make a diorama, being sure to include important details such as a tree in which a leopard might store a killed animal.

• The leopard relies on camouflage to keep hidden from its prey. This tactic is also used by many other animals, including humans. Design a costume that would camouflage you in the woods; on the seashore; in the mountains.

NOTES

1. Ronald M. Nowak and John L. Paradiso, *Walker's Mammals of the World*, 4th ed., vol. 2 (Baltimore, Md.: Johns Hopkins University Press, 1983), 1090.

RESOURCE BIBLIOGRAPHY

Books

Adamson, Joy. *Queen of Shaba: The Story of an African Leopard*. New York: Harcourt Brace Jovanovich, 1980.
This book features Penny, a leopard raised by the author of the well-known work, *Born Free*. The book features anecdotal information about leopards in general and this one leopard in particular. The life of Penny is chronicled from when she was a cub through the time she became a mother. Considerable scientific data is collected from this sample of one.

Corbett, Jim. *Man-Eaters of India*. New York: Oxford University Press, 1957.
Jim Corbett recounts several adventures in which he hunted down man-eating tigers and leopards. Adventure is the primary thrust of the book, though some natural history is occasionally included. The expeditions described are sensational, turn-of-the-century accounts of sports hunting.

Dorliae, Peter G. *Animals Mourn for Da Leopard and Other West African Tales*. New York: Bobbs-Merrill, 1970.
These are bold tales illustrated with bold art. This little book delivers a powerful and somewhat humorous view of relationships among people and animals. Ten stories and a few proverbs are included.

Elliot, Geraldine. *Where the Leopard Passes: A Book of African Folk Tales*. New York: Schocken Books, 1968.
This book of African folktales centers around the antics and interactions of the animals of Africa. The author uses authentic folktales and authentic (though sometimes difficult to pronounce) African names of animals.

Goss, Linda. *The Baby Leopard: A "How and Why" Story*. New York: Bantam Books, 1989.
This original story for young readers was inspired by West African folktales about how the leopard got its spots.

Kipling, Rudyard. *Just So Stories for Little Children*. New York: Chatham River Press, a Division of Arlington House, 1978.
In the storytelling tradition, using words that are meant to be said aloud, Kipling tickles the fancy of a child's mind. Using colorful language, characters, names (such as "Slow-Solid Tortoise" and "Sickly-Prickly Hedgehog") and places such as the "High Veldt" and "the great grey-green, greasy Limpopo River," Kipling answers questions that only a child could ask concerning such topics as how the leopard got its spots and how the camel got his hump.

Lester, Julius. *How Many Spots Does a Leopard Have? And Other Tales*. New York: Scholastic, 1989.
A collection of twelve African and Jewish folk tales. Illustrated by David Shannon.

Line, Les, and Edward R. Ricciuti. "Bold Hunters." In *The Audubon Society Book of Wild Cats*. New York: Harry N. Abrams, 1985.
The authors trace the reemergence in Israel of the Sinai leopard (*Panthera pardus jarvisi*), an animal thought to have been extinct. The natural history of leopards in general is discussed.

Nowak, Ronald M., and John L. Paradiso. *Walker's Mammals of the World*, 4th ed. vol. 2. Baltimore, Md.: Johns Hopkins University Press, 1983, 1089-91.
This encyclopedia of mammals is among the most extensive available. Full details on hundreds of mammals are given. The section concerning *Panthera pardus* contains photographs that help the reader to develop a real feeling for the animal being described.

Rabinowitz, Alan. *Chasing the Dragon's Tail: The Struggle to Save Thailand's Wild Cats*. New York: Doubleday, 1991.
Activities of the Huai Kha Khaeng Wildlife Sanctuary are detailed. Problems involved in the wild animal trade work against saving the large cats of Thailand.

Walker, Barbara K. *The Dancing Palm Tree and Other Nigerian Folktales*. Lubbock, Tex.: Texas Tech University Press, 1990.
The author recounts eleven Nigerian tales first told to her by Olawale Idewu, a Nigerian student in a midwestern university, to whom she dedicated the book. Nigerian stories are meant to educate as well as entertain and there is usually a moral to each story. Exquisite woodcuts and color printing accompany the gentle text and together make this a lovely book.

Magazine Articles

Cahalane, Victor H. "King of Cats and His Court." *National Geographic* 83 (February 1943): 217-59.

This interesting article, although old, is not really dated in its exposition of the natural history of the big cats. It does not address the aspect of endangerment of these animals because that was not a great concern in the 1940s. However, the entertaining text and exciting paintings make this a fine resource.

California Condors

AGE OF THE CONDOR

Script by Glenn McGlathery

he young chick and the old male condor sat perched on a limb in their cage in the San Diego Zoo. The large male preened his feathers as the chick attempted to mimic the actions. The sun was well above the horizon and the day promised to be as nice as almost all the days in this southern California climate. The splendid sun warmed the tired old bones of Xonal, now in his fortieth year. The light breeze stirred the spring leaves in the trees in the spotlessly clean enclosure.

"Tell me, grandfather," said the chick, "what it was like when I was hatched."

"I've told you that story a thousand times, Molloko. Why do you want to hear it again?"

"I just do, grandfather. I never get tired of hearing about it."

"Luckily," chuckled the old bird, as he placed his large wing around the chick, "I never get tired of telling it. Your being hatched was a great moment in the life of our family. We had wondered so long if we were the end of our line. There were so few left in the flock and no egg laid since we had been in these cages had ever hatched. So it was with great joy and anticipation that we watched you peck your way out of the shell and into this fine cage."

Molloko noticed a certain sarcasm as Xonal said the word *fine*.

"Isn't it a fine cage, grandfather?"

"Well, yes, as cages go, but once we were free to fly where we wanted."

"Just what does freedom mean, grandfather?" questioned Molloko.

"It means you don't have a cage around you. You can fly for a hundred miles if you wish."

"Fly a hundred miles?" asked Molloko, as if he didn't have a grasp of the concept.

"Further, even. There were no boundaries in the old days. Before I was captured, I stayed pretty much in the San Joaquin Valley north of here, but I could range as far as I wanted," Xonal said dreamily.

"But why would you want to fly so far? Food is always close to us. All we have to do is jump down off our perches and pick it up. We seem so well cared for here. We can fly here."

"Oh, Molloko, there are advantages, no doubt. But then, you haven't known the thrill of soaring at ten thousand feet, of finding a food supply on your own, of going hundreds of miles in any direction you choose. I just remember when we were on our own. It was so different then."

"Tell me, grandfather," shouted Molloko enthusiastically.

"When I was free, we were few. Our relatives lived nearby and we had contact, but our numbers were falling. I remember counting only fifty, then forty, then thirty," continued the old bird, his eyes beginning to mist. "I heard of great numbers in the great long ago, of thousands who ranged the whole of the continent. Our stories go back hundreds of thousands of years, to when the uprights didn't live in houses and drive cars on those crowded freeways. The uprights didn't bother us then. They were too busy seeing to their own survival. Mostly, the uprights left us alone, but one flock of the uprights worshiped us as gods. Xol, they called us. We took the spirits of their departed to heaven on our strong backs, using our huge wings. Another upright flock took a great interest in us, but they did not see us as gods—they wanted our great feathers to make capes to use in their dancing. Many of our ancestors perished at the hands of these people. Even so, there was much game and space and our numbers remained. But then ... but then ..." the giant bird trailed off.

"But then what, grandfather? What happened? Why do you seem so sad?" asked the little bird. His wings drooped as his own eyes started to mist also.

"Many things happened, all at once, it seems," said Xonal, his voice steadying and his posture returning to a proud stance. "More and more uprights began to live on this land. They started on one great ocean and moved to the other with incredible speed. The numbers of the uprights who were here first started to diminish, like our own numbers, and the uprights who were new began to take charge. They came west in wagons, on horseback, on foot, and later on noisy land and air machines. These uprights brought their own cattle and hunted the antelope and deer and other animals that competed for the food of their livestock. When their cattle died and we flocked to feast on them as we had on dead wild animals, the uprights thought we had killed the cattle, so they killed us as if we were poachers. They used our big hollow feathers to carry gold dust and hunted us relentlessly. Our numbers began to decrease dramatically. Our food supply became more and more scarce as the new uprights moved in. Some cleared the land and planted crops, not even giving us access to the few cattle that died. Our range became more and more confined as our numbers began to drop. We finally realized that we weren't going to survive many more years at this alarming rate, but it seemed too late to do anything about it. Then the captures began."

"Tell me about your capture, grandfather. How did it happen?" begged the young condor. "Did you put up a fight? Weren't you just scared to death?"

"Scared, yes. I didn't know what was happening. I simply landed on what looked like a good meal when all of a sudden this giant net dropped down from the sky and I was hopelessly entangled. Squirm as I might, I couldn't get free. I saw three or four uprights rushing at me. What did they want? To kill me because they thought I had killed some of their cattle? To pluck my great feathers for some reason? I had no idea what was happening and I thought I was going to die. But it didn't happen. I went to sleep from something the uprights did and when I woke up I was here with a few other condors.

"Snabul, over there, was here when I arrived," he said, gesturing to a lone condor preening on a branch in a tree beside them. "So was Monkol and Xendel. Prodol, Belchor, and Yemonal all came later, the same way that I did. But you, Molloko, are different. You were born here, not brought from the outside like the rest of us. I know that the uprights are almost as excited about you as we are."

"What will happen to us, grandfather? Will we ever be free? Will we soar again above the great valleys?"

"I think some of us will, Molloko. I think you will. The uprights didn't capture us to harm us, but to save us. Someday we might all be free and be able to have our families once again in the wild. You might be in the same valley where I soared as a young adult, or you might be set free in a land I have never seen. When you are free and soaring, Molloko, I want you to think of me, of all of us, those you know and those ancestors of whom you have only heard. Remember that we have a long history on this land. We were the last thing that the very last woolly mammoth saw before it died, the last vision of the last saber-toothed cat. We've outlived them all, at least until now. Be proud of our heritage, Molloko," concluded Xonal.

"You know that I am, grandfather. Thank you for telling me the story again. When I have my own grandchildren in the wild, I'll tell them the stories you have told me and make them as proud as I am."

► ● ◄

FOLKLORE

The California condor had a relatively small range, even in ancient times, but did not escape the attention of the people. The great soaring birds seemed like spirits of the dead to early Indians. They were known as "birds of thunder" and thought to bring the rain when they flapped their enormous wings.

The great bird was revered by the Chumash Indian tribe. These Indians called the bird Xol, which literally means "god." They believed that departed spirits rode the backs of the giant birds to paradise in the afterlife.

The Miwok Indians also paid homage to the California condor. The bird was adored for its extraordinary strength and stamina. That the condor could soar for about an hour without flapping its wings was awe-inspiring. Condor skins with feathers in place were used in dance rituals. The dancer donned the skin, putting his head through the hole where the condor's head had been. The dancer's head was painted to resemble the bright naked head of the condor. The dancer waved his arms as if flying and flexed his knees in a gentle motion as he danced around making the condor's hissing sound.

Eighteenth-century Spanish explorers landed at an Indian village in what is now Monterey, California. There they saw that the natives had killed a condor, stuffed it with straw, and seemed to worship it as an idol.

Westward-moving pioneers held a variety of erroneous notions and superstitions about the California condor. They believed that they not only carried diseases but also carried away calves, lambs, and sometimes human babies.

DISCUSSION

Description

California condors (*Gymnogyps californianus*) rank among the world's largest flying birds. Adults weigh almost 20 pounds (about 9 kilograms) and have a wingspan of over 9 feet (2.7 meters). Adults are black except for white markings under the wings and on the edges of the wings. The featherless head and neck are predominantly red or orange. Sex cannot be determined by size or plumage. Birds mature physically in five or six years, but do not reach sexual maturity until they are about eight years old. Juveniles have grayish-black heads and gradually acquire adult coloration. The wing linings of immature birds are mottled. The California condor is a member of the family *Cathartidae*, a family of seven species that includes a close relative, the Andean condor, and the turkey vulture.

Behavior

The California condor is a scavenger that feeds on dead deer, elk, pronghorn antelope, cattle, and smaller mammals. The bird has no natural enemies and can live as long as forty-five years. They are phenomenal fliers, able to reach speeds of 60 miles per hour (95 kilometers per hour) and may range over 200 miles each day between their nests and food. The female condor lays a single egg that hatches after about eight weeks. Both parents share the incubation duty. The young chick demands care from both parents for the first two months of life. The chick flies in about six months but does not become fully independent for about eighteen months.

Habitat

The California condor nests in caves and crevices in isolated, rocky cliffs along the Pacific coast and nearby mountain ranges. It roosts in tall trees near foraging grounds. It spends most of the morning preening and grooming and then flies off in search of carrion (dead flesh), returning to the roost at night. The birds forage in open grassland, primarily in the foothills surrounding the southern San Joaquin Valley of California. They require fairly open terrain for feeding because they need a long distance (runway) for taking off and landing. The habitat of the condor in recent years has been confined to about nine counties in southern California, including Monterey, San Benito, San Luis Obispo, Santa Barbara, Ventura, Los Angeles, Kings, Tulare, and Kern.

Historic Range

The fossil record reveals that the California condor lived 100,000 years ago in the time of the saber-toothed tigers and woolly mammoths. Then the species ranged over most of western North America, from British Columbia to northern Baja California, and along the eastern coast to Florida. Condors nested in western Texas, Arizona, and New Mexico until about 2,000 years ago. They lived in the Pacific Northwest until the 1800s, when the population is estimated to have been about 500, and in northern Baja California until the early 1930s. Their area had shrunk to that previously described by the 1960s, when fewer than sixty individuals survived. By the early 1980s, only about twenty-five birds survived (see fig. 7.1, page 88). In 1986, only five individuals existed in the wild.[1] In 1982 eight wild condors were captured and brought to the San Diego Zoo to join with a condor captured in 1967. The winter of 1984-1985 proved disastrous for the species, as four of the last five breeding pairs in the wild disappeared. At that time the U.S. Fish and Wildlife Service decided to capture the remaining wild condors for a breeding program. The action was quite controversial. Some scientists considered the capture premature. Others considered it timely if the species were to be given a chance of survival. The last free condor was captured on the Bitter Creek National Wildlife Refuge on April 19, 1987. Currently the total breeding population is twenty-seven. Fourteen birds are in the San Diego Wild Animal Park and thirteen are at the Los Angeles Zoo. Counting chicks and juveniles, there were 52 condors in captivity as of October 1991.[2]

Reasons for Near-Extinction and Attempts to Help

It is not known exactly why the condor population shrank to such a fragile number. Reproduction failure has been suggested, since mating pairs produce only a single egg every other year. Certainly, factors introduced by human habitation of the same land, such as electrocution by power lines, are also responsible. The use of pesticides undoubtedly played a role, as concentrations of pesticides in condor prey and the birds' own tissues led to thinning and breakage of eggshells. Because these birds feed on carrion, condors ingest any poisons that killed their prey, such as cyanide or strychnine. They also suffer lead poisoning when they eat lead shot remaining in the bodies of animals killed by hunters. Further, as the condors' territory became settled, food became more scarce. Cattle ranchers aggressively hunted predators, such as wolves and coyotes, and controlled competitors, such as deer and antelope, so naturally occurring carcasses became increasingly rare. At first condors had a fairly good supply of dead domestic cattle, but two factors all but eliminated that food supply. First, ranchers, seeing flocks of condors on the carcasses of dead cattle, incorrectly assumed that the condors had killed the

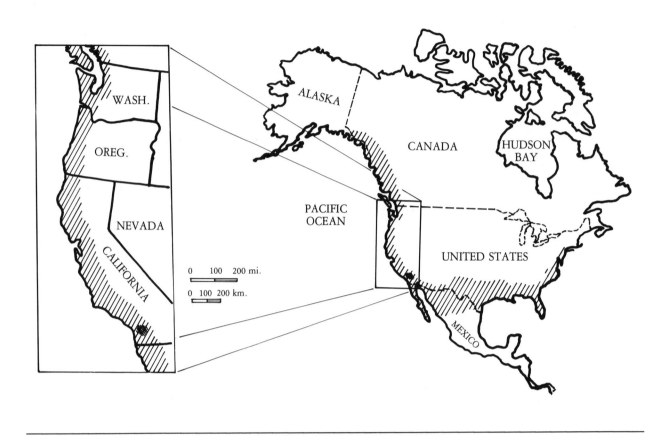

Fig. 7.1. Present and historic ranges of the California condor.

cattle, so they began shooting the birds. Second, the rise of agriculture in the rich San Joaquin Valley of California limited the number of cattle ranches, forcing the condors to travel far from their roosts to find food.

The California condor has now retreated to its last refuge, in captivity at the Los Angeles Zoo and the San Diego Wild Animal Park. The breeding population stands at about thirty, as of the end of 1991, and a captive breeding program seems to be working, albeit slowly. The first condor chick ever conceived in captivity was hatched at the San Diego Wild Animal Park in April 1988. The chick was named *Molloko*, which is a Maidu Indian word meaning *condor*. A second chick was hatched in April 1989 and additional eggs are being incubated and hatched in an ongoing program to support the condor population.

Despite these successes, many questions remain. The chicks are being hatched by a very small flock of individuals (sixteen males and eleven females), thus raising concerns that the gene pool may be too limited to produce healthy offspring. Sexual maturity for the new members takes seven or eight years, assuming they survive that long, and even then inbreeding remains a real problem.

Other concerns surround the eventual goal of reintroducing the condor to the wild. In fact, there was much heated debate about removing the last wild birds: one faction wanted to leave them in the wild and find other ways to solve the problem of their declining numbers. The questions now are whether, when, and where to release individuals back into their native habitat. How many should be reintroduced? Do the conditions that led to their near-extinction still exist? Can reintroduced birds avoid these hazards to reestablish wild breeding populations? How many should remain in captivity, to ensure the survival of the species? Can birds that were captured or were reared in captivity survive in the wild? (The rearing of condor chicks in captivity is still very much a human-intensive job, although great pains are taken to mimic the parents' appearance and surroundings that wild chicks would experience.)

On January 15, 1992, a pair of California condors was released in the Los Padres National Forest in California, in the hope that they would reestablish their territories and resume their historical place in the wild. Meanwhile, a research study is in progress in southern California, using captive-bred Andean condors, a close relative of the California condor. This study may give some direction to the reintroduction program. Whether the California condor will survive, either in the wild or ultimately in captivity, is still unknown.

CONDOR ACTIVITIES

Condors and the Environment

* Prepare a shoebox-sized display that shows where a California condor might nest or roost. Include a pair of condors and possible prey. A good place to get ideas is in a museum of natural history.

* Prepare a map of North America. Show the range of the California condor in the years 200, 1800, 1960, 1980, 1985, and 1990.

* California condors existed in the Ice Age in the Pleistocene epoch. They dined on the carcasses of woolly mammoths and saber-toothed tigers. Prepare a condor's eyewitness account of the environment on a typical day in the Ice Age. *The Great Ice Age* by Christopher Maynard will give you some ideas.

* Research the conflict between the California condor and the immigrants who settled the western United States. Summarize your research through a presentation of your choice.

* An article in *The Denver Post*, on Sunday, October 21, 1990, suggests that the Gray Ranch near Animas, New Mexico, would be an ideal site for the release of California condors, since the fossil record indicates that the birds were once numerous in this locale and there are currently few people and plentiful game. Research other locations for the release of the birds.

Condors as an Endangered Species

- Write a journal article making a case for preservation of the California condor or taking the position that nature should run its course.

- Imagine a pair of California condors sitting on a roost, contemplating the fact that their species is dying and that they are becoming extinct. Write a dialogue of the conversation between the two birds. Use the readers' theatre script that follows in this chapter to get ideas, but develop your own script.

- Write to request information about the California condor or send a statement of your opinion of what should be done about the species:

  Regional Office of Endangered Species
  U.S. Fish and Wildlife Service
  Lloyd 500 Building, Suite 1692
  500 NE Multnomah Street
  Portland, OR 97232

- Research the amount of public money spent on helping the California condor survive extinction. How much is this for each individual in the United States? Discuss the topic, "Should public funds be used to save the California condor from extinction?"

Condors and the Arts

- The resource book, *A Vanishing Thunder*, describes a dance of the Miwok Indians in which they pay homage to the condor. (See page 86 for a summary of this ritual.) From the description in the book, choreograph the dance, using appropriate costumes and props. Prepare an introduction that explains the dance and perform both for an audience.

- Construct a full-scale papier-mâché model of the California condor.

- The California condor is depicted in cave paintings of the Chumash Indian tribe, who called the condor *Xol* (meaning god) and believed their spirits were carried to heaven on the condor's wings. Research other peoples that have used a bird as the center of their religion.

Readers' Theatre

The Last Days of the Condor

Cast of characters:

Narrator
Seven California condors:
    Ivan
    Bono
    Sobon
    Xonon (the youngest)
    Pegasus
    Doban
    Xol (the oldest)

Narrator: The scene is a high mountain ledge overlooking the San Joaquin Valley in southern California. The seven remaining condors in the wild are gathered, watching the convoy of trucks of their would-be captors snake along the valley floor. The convoy stops, people get out, and a flurry of activity begins as the workers erect a huge net west of an open pasture. The condors speak.

Ivan: Just look at that! See them work so hard? What do you think the uprights are doing today?

Bono: They're up to no good. You can be sure of that.

All: Yeah!

Sobon: Just wait. More of us will disappear. It seems our numbers always get smaller after the uprights work like this.

Ivan: So it seems. As I count, we're the only ones left. The last of a proud flock of condors that was here long before the uprights.

Xonon: What happens to us—I mean, after we're captured by the uprights?

Ivan: You're too young to remember much, Xonon. Your own mother was taken away by the uprights. She put up such a fight! All the screeching, clawing, and biting—I saw it all. You were still a chick then. They took Lorelei away in a big truck with a cage on the back. I soared as near as I dared, but I was afraid they might take me, too. I followed them to a large cage where I think I saw many of our flock. Who knows what happens after that?

Pegasus: Don't scare the child, Ivan. She's been through enough. At least we know her mother is alive and seems to be treated well.

Sobon: How can you say "treated well"? They are taken from us, never to soar again! If you are not free, can it be said that you are treated well?

Pegasus: How well are we? We are almost to the point of starvation. We have to fly a couple of hundred miles to get any food at all and then we are lucky to find a small coyote that has died. Even then, we often get sick from the thing that killed the coyote. The days are gone when the meat supply was plentiful and we didn't have to work so much to find a meal.

Doban: Are you saying, Pegasus, that you would trade places with your brothers and sisters captured by the uprights? Would you give up your freedom, as hard as it is to live, to the uprights?

Pegasus: At least I could eat regularly. No, Doban, I cherish my freedom, but I am beginning to see that our days are numbered, free or not.

Xol: Don't despair, my friends. We might make a comeback yet.

Ivan: You're senile, old one. What are you? Forty? Forty-five? Don't you see what is happening? In your lifetime you have seen our number decrease from forty or fifty to just the seven of us, plus, of course, the captives in the cages. Do you really think we can make a comeback? Return to our former glory?

Xol: Oh, we've been through a lot. We've been revered as gods, hunted as cattle killers, and killed for our feathers, but we're still here. We may not be many, but we're still here.

Ivan: For how long, old one? For how long?

Xol: Who knows the answer to that? Maybe the uprights are helping us, taking us away to protect the precious few of us left.

Doban: It sounds like you want to be captured, like Pegasus. Why don't the two of you just fly down and right into the cages on their trucks?

Xol: Just hold on, Doban. I'm not saying I want to be captured, but I don't want to see our numbers dwindle even more, either. (Pause) Look at the uprights. What are they doing now?

Ivan: Are you also blind, old one? The uprights are taking that dead cow off their truck. They'll leave it in the field for us. Then when we land and eat some of it they'll swoop down with their nets. They don't think we know what is happening. See how they've put the carcass next to those trees? They know we'll glide in and land on the carcass. They know, too, that we'll have to take off the same way we came in. See the net they're setting up to trap us as we take off? I've seen this lots of times before.

Sobon: Oh, you're right, Ivan. That's what they're up to.

Xonon: You mean if I fly down there the uprights will capture me and take me away? Maybe I'll get to see my mother.

Doban: Don't even think about it, Xonon. You might get hurt. They might kill you. They might take you to a different place from your mother. You can't trust the uprights.

Pegasus:	We don't know about that, Doban. We've never seen the uprights kill any of us. They seem more concerned with our safety than our death.
Doban:	Think what you like, Pegasus. Whatever happens, I'll stay here and watch it all. You wouldn't catch me down there flying into their trap.
Narrator:	Most of the other condors seem to agree with the assessment by Doban and Ivan and are content to stay on their perches, preening themselves and considering their afternoon flight for food. Sobon agrees to soar first as a scout and to let the others know the distance and direction they will have to go for food today. Shortly after noon, Doban becomes airborne, riding the thermals to heights of over two miles.
Xonon:	I hope he finds something, enough for all of us. I am so hungry.
Bono:	Me, too. I haven't eaten for three days, at least nothing substantial. Even then, I could only find a small squirrel.
Ivan:	Just relax. Maybe today will be different. There's always that cow in the valley down there (chuckles).
Narrator:	Eventually Sobon returns. Spirits fall as the birds receive the bad news.
Sobon:	Nothing worth flying out for. Sorry. I saw some ravens and eagles circling to the north about twenty miles away. When I got close I could see that they were circling a small deer that already had dozens of birds on it. We'll just have to take our chances on whatever small game hasn't been spotted yet. Good luck.
Pegasus:	I'm not even going out. It takes more energy than the energy we'll get from the little bit of food we find.
Ivan:	If you keep this up, Pegasus, you'll just starve to death. Is that what you want?
Pegasus:	Is that what any of us want? We're so near the end now, I'm thinking of sampling the cow that the uprights brought.
Bono:	No, Pegasus. Our number will drop even lower. We love you and don't want to lose you.
Pegasus:	You'll lose me soon enough to starvation. Who knows? I might be able to eat some of the cow and escape too. I've sized up the situation down there. I see where their net is and I think I can gain altitude faster than they think I can. I'm going to try. Who's coming with me?
Xol:	I think I will, Pegasus. I don't really think your plan will work but I have nothing to lose.
Xonon:	Me, too. I think I'll see my mother if I'm captured. If I'm not captured, at least I will have had a good meal.
Ivan:	You're all talking crazily. You don't have a chance.

Pegasus: At least if we don't make it we won't be competing with you for food. You'll have more to eat after we're gone. But I think we'll make it.

Ivan: Well, then, if your mind is made up, good luck!

Narrator: The three birds take off and head straight for the carcass that has been brought by the researchers from the animal park in San Diego. As they glide in, they see that only a few crows are clustered on the large body. After the long glide, they land awkwardly near the carcass, scaring the crows away. They hop up on the mound of meat and begin to eat, taking in large beakfuls of food that begin to satisfy their great hunger. Eagerly they tear at flesh until there seems to be more bones than meat. Warily they watch the researchers, who stand about trying to hide and saying nothing. They eye the giant net that now lies on the ground, but which they know will be lifted on great pulleys by the uprights when the condors start to fly away. At last, having eaten their fill, Pegasus speaks:

Pegasus: Well, this is it. Let's make a run for it.

Narrator: The giant wings of the three magnificent birds begin to beat furiously. Very slowly, they begin to gain altitude as the researchers quickly lift the net. Just as the researchers had predicted and the condors had dreaded, it becomes obvious that the great birds are not going to clear the net. As the condors become entangled, the net lowers. Gingerly the researchers approach the helpless birds and gently take them to the waiting trucks.

Xol: It was worth a try. At least I'm full and I can see that the uprights mean us no harm.

Pegasus: I have no regrets. We were doomed either way. Maybe our luck will change and we can make a comeback with the help of the uprights.

Xonon: Maybe I'll get to see my mother again.

NOTES

1. "Condor Breakthrough," *U.S. News and World Report* 104 (May 9, 1988): 18.

2. "California Condors to Fly Free," *Weekly Reader* 70 (October 11, 1991): 4-5.

RESOURCE BIBLIOGRAPHY

Books

Darlington, David. *In Condor Country*. Boston: Houghton Mifflin, 1987.
   The natural history of San Luis Obispo County (California) and its famous endangered residents are discussed.

Halliday, Tim. *Vanishing Birds: Their Natural History and Conservation*. New York: Holt, Rinehart & Winston, 1978.
   The author gives good technical and popular information about extinct and endangered bird species of the world. Well-done drawings and color plates give excellent illustrations of these vanishing or extinct birds.

Matthews, John R., ed. *The Official World Wildlife Fund Guide to Endangered Species*. Vol. 2. Washington, D.C.: Walton Beacham, 1990.
This book is an excellent reference concerning endangered species. The entry for each species treated includes description, behavior, habitat, distribution information, and status. The reference is a must for students interested in factual information about various species.

Maynard, Christopher. *The Great Ice Age*. New York: Warwick Press, 1979.
Chronicles the Ice Age, including geology and animals. Good reading for the intermediate-grade-level student.

Stoutenburg, Adrien. "The California Condor and the American Egret." In *A Vanishing Thunder*, 73-91. Garden City, N.Y.: Natural History Press, 1967.
This book gives interesting information on a half-dozen extinct and threatened American birds, including the California condor. A history of the condor is given, along with suggestions of problems that might have pushed the bird toward extinction.

Magazine Articles

Brower, Kenneth. "The Naked Vulture and the Thinking Ape." *Atlantic Monthly* 252 (October 1983): 70-80.
This very scholarly article reviews the issues that surrounded the debate among biologists about what to do with the remaining wild condors. One camp favored captive breeding and the other camp bitterly opposed this position, favoring instead protecting the bird in its natural environment.

"California Condors to Fly Free." *Weekly Reader* 70 (October 11, 1991): 4-5.
This article briefly recounts the California condor's struggle for survival and discusses plans for releasing the birds into the wild.

"Condor Breakthrough." *U.S. News and World Report* 104 (May 9, 1988): 18.
The article recounts the hatching of Molloko, the first California condor conceived in captivity. The existence of the egg was considered miraculous by many, since it was widely believed that condors would not mate in captivity.

Crawford, Mark. "Condor Agreement Reached." *Science* 229 (September 20, 1985): 1248.
Crawford's article details an agreement between the California Fish and Game Commission, the Audubon Society, and the U.S. Department of the Interior. The basic agreement was to capture some of the remaining condors but allow a few to remain free to help with the assimilation of currently captive birds that would eventually be returned to the wild.

_____. "The Last Days of the Wild Condor?" *Science* 229 (August 30, 1985): 844-45.
This article summarizes the issues surrounding the debate that raged over whether to capture the few remaining condors and attempt to breed them in captivity or to attempt a less intrusive measure.

Gorman, Christine (as reported by Paul Krueger). "The Biggest Shell Game in Town." *Time* 131 (May 16, 1988): 72.
This article details the birth of Molloko, the first condor hatched in captivity. The captive pair mated in January. The four-and-one-half-inch-long egg was laid on March 3. The egg was incubated and on April 29, 1988, Molloko appeared, after considerable help from staff at the San Diego Wild Animal Park. Some of the history of the condor's endangerment as well as current recovery efforts are treated.

Gwynne, Peter, and Jeff B. Copeland. "Lo, the California Condor." *Newsweek* 95 (May 26, 1980): 58.
The debate on capturing wild condors is discussed. Favoring capture and supervised breeding were the U.S. Fish and Wildlife Service and the National Audubon Society. On the other side of the controversy were Friends of the Earth and the Sierra Club, which wanted to study the species further before intervening.

Hudson, Jeffrey S. "Controversy Over the California Condor." *Sierra* 64 (July/August 1979): 52-55.
This article looks at issues concerning whether to capture remaining condors and further their species by breeding them in captivity or to leave them in the wild and seek some other intervention. The Sierra Club's position favored captive breeding but endorsed no particular plan.

Lang, John S., Pamela Ellis-Simons, and Elisabeth Blaug. "Caged: The Last Wild Condor." *U.S. News and World Report* 101 (May 4, 1987): 62-63.
The article recounts the history of the condor, the tragedy of its shrinking numbers, and the decision of the U.S. Fish and Wildlife Service to capture all the remaining birds after the disastrous winter of 1984-1985, during which six birds disappeared without a trace.

"Last Days of the Condor." *U.S. News and World Report* 100 (January 27, 1986): 5.
This short news article reports on the capture of the first of six condors left in the wild, this one taken because she was suffering from poisoning caused by lead shot that she swallowed. It is suggested that unless a way is found to reintroduce the bird into nature, California condors may soon and forever be viewed behind wire enclosures in zoos and animal parks.

"Meet Molloko—One Ugly Chick But Beautiful News for California's Threatened Condors." *People Weekly* 29 (May 16, 1988): 48.
The care of the $20 million egg (so called because of the amount of money spent on the condor recovery program) that contained the first condor conceived in captivity is detailed. The article reveals that simulated maternal sounds were played for the emerging chick to help encourage it in the hatching process. Human intervention was used to help the chick in its 60-hour emergence ordeal.

Peterson, Russ. "Saving the Condor." *Audubon* 86 (January 1984): 4.
This editorial by the president of the Audubon Society applauds the effort and seeming success of the condor recovery (capture) program in which seven individuals were captured in 1983 alone. Their capture brought the number of captive individuals to nine, a dramatic change for the formerly solitary Topa Topa, longtime resident of the Los Angeles Zoo.

Weisburg, S. "Happy Birthday, Condor Chick." *Science News* 133 (May 7, 1988): 295.
 The article details the hatching of Molloko, the first California condor chick conceived in captivity, although not the first hatched. Over a dozen chicks have been hatched from eggs taken from the wild.

Wells, Claudia. "Love Among the Condors." *Time* 118 (September 21, 1981): 70.
 This article traces some of the history of the condor on the Pacific coast and reports the issues involved in the debate over whether to capture remaining birds, let nature take its course, or intervene in the birds' environment.

Northern Spotted Owls

HOW MR. OWL GOT HIS STRANGE VOICE

A Louisiana Tale

Once upon a time Mr. Owl was the greatest of singers. He could sing any number of fine songs, some short, some long, all beautiful. Mr. Owl was the envy of the woods with his large collection of wonderful songs. Other birds came to him for singing lessons. He taught the whippoorwill its great mournful song and the bobwhite the short perky song that has become its trademark. The finch learned its beautiful melodies sitting on a branch next to Mr. Owl. The mockingbird learned its vast repertoire from the wise, talented, and patient owl.

But, as things sometimes happen, something brought an end to Mr. Owl's happy days of joyful singing. He and Miz Owl had a nice and respectable nest-house in the crotch of a big sycamore tree, where they spent many pleasurable hours. One night Miz Owl decided she needed to go out, so she told Mr. Owl to stay home and take care of the nest and the little ones. This suited Mr. Owl just fine for a little while, but then he got itchy feet and wanted to go out, too. So he took his fiddle and went out for a night on the town to see what he could see and do what he could do.

Just as soon as Mr. Owl left the next-house, Miz Cuckoo came along. When she saw what a fine place it was, she decided to move in and set up housekeeping. She promptly laid an egg there and then decided to go out and get some nice curtains and a rug to help decorate her new house. It was about this time that Miz Owl returned.

Miz Owl was horrified to find a strange egg in her nest-house and was more than a little curious to know where it had come from. Mr. Owl was no help at all in this matter, so, because of the failed trust and on general principles, Miz Owl threw him out.

Mr. Owl went in search of the bird who had laid the egg and brought him his misfortune. He went everywhere he knew searching for the mysterious homewrecker and asking always, "Who? Who? Who?" In fact, he asked "who" for so long that this became his new song. He forgot all the melodies he once knew, the grand melodies that were the envy of all the other birds in the woods. Also, because he was ashamed of the mess he had made with Miz Owl and all, he started to hide during the daytime and come out only at night. Even now, on many nights you can hear his sad, almost brokenhearted question, "Who? Who? Who?"

▶●◀

FOLKLORE

Owls have a checkered reputation in folklore. Sometimes their presence bodes well and sometimes it means ill, but throughout history the owl has fascinated people. When we hear the plaintive hoot of the owl or catch a quick glimpse of it, we pay attention and almost always instinctively attach some significance to the encounter. According to various folk traditions, such a chance meeting brings good luck or bad, portends good or bad weather, or represents wisdom or folly. The mystery humans associate with the owl and the contradictory omens we assign all contribute to the legendary status of the owl in folklore, literature, and our lives.

Human fascination with owls seems timeless. Prehistoric rock drawings of owls can be seen from France to Australia. The tales of owls told around campfires have travelled through generations and across continents and seem to encompass the polar notions of fear and joy, happiness and dread, death and life.

This strange—many think unnatural—bird is different from other birds in many respects. Its appearance is quite striking with a face more like a cat than a bird. Its behavior is likewise strange. It can turn its neck almost a full circle. Settlers on the western plains of the United States were fascinated by the burrowing owl because it always faced anyone approaching. Tall tales told of circling the small bird and causing it to wring its own neck. In reality, the burrowing owl makes such a quick head reverse that it is barely detectable. The owl sees in the dark, flies in the dark, and has a call unlike that of any other bird.

The song of the owl is the theme of the little story that opens this chapter. A Spanish legend relates that the owl once had a sweet song, but after its presence at the crucifixion of Christ could only repeat the word *cruz* (Spanish for *cross*). The first-century Roman naturalist, Pliny, observed that the owl sings nine different notes.

The tyrant Agathocles of Syracuse ordered owls released among his troops before an attack on the Carthaginians. The birds settled on shields and helmets, boosting the morale of the soldiers. Pliny suggested that carrying the heart of an owl in battle heartens the bearer and enhances his performance. A chief of the Pima Indians sought assistance from the owl in his battle with the Apaches. The Tlingit Indians rushed into battle hooting like owls to give themselves confidence and to rattle their enemies. The owl's reputation as hunter is a characteristic revered by most tribes, particularly its ability to strike prey noiselessly and surely.

The owl symbol is very strong among Native Americans. Navaho Indian legend has the creator, Nayenezgani, telling an owl upon creating it that "in days to come men will listen to your voice to know what will be their future." For an Apache to dream of an owl foretold the dreamer's death. The Kwakiutl Indians considered owls to be the reincarnated souls of people and, therefore, not to be harmed. The Lenape Indians believed that if one dreamt of an owl it would become a guardian. According to some tribes of California, the Great Horned Owl captured the souls of the dead and carried them to the other world. The Mojave Indians of Arizona thought that they became owls after death for an interim or transition stage. An Achomawi Indian legend from northern California tells about the owl setting out after the flood to see if he could find any spark of fire after the waters had extinguished all the fires of the world. After a time the owl returned, reporting that he had seen smoke in the west coming from steam baths. The next day everyone started west carrying cedar bark vessels in which they brought fire back to their homes. A Penobscot Indian tale has a snowy owl being sent out in search of water, finding it, and being crowned chief of his village. Many other Native American stories and legends feature the owl as a death omen. "I heard the owl call my name" is an often-used metaphor for impending death.

The owl was sacred to the Teton Sioux. Their medicine men received their powers through dreams as clear as the sight of an owl. In recognition of this power, the Tetons wore owl feathers. The Pima Indians gave an owl feather to their dying in an effort to help them reach the owl who awaited their spirits.

Feathers figure prominently in many legends about owls. A legend from the Middle East tells that people originally had feathers and wings but no fire. An owl nearby had flint and iron which he used to make a fire and keep warm because he had no feathers. One day the leader of the tribe met the owl and struck a deal so that people got the materials for making fire and the owl got feathers and the ability to fly. The owl was overly fond of his feathers, according to another ancient folktale. The wren had flown too close to the sun and had scorched its feathers. Other birds in their generosity had given some of their feathers to replenish the wren, but not the owl. This is why, the tale concludes, the owl now spends the daytime hours in its hole: the owl is ashamed and the other birds angry because of the owl's selfishness. John Keats makes reference to the bountiful plumage of the owl in his poem, *The Eve of St. Agnes*:

> St. Agnes Eve—Ah, bitter chill it was!
> The owl for all its feathers was a-cold.[1]

The little owl (*Athene noctua*) was the symbol of the Greek goddess Athene (Minerva to the Romans), goddess of wisdom. The owl is associated with Bacchus's favorite plant, the ivy. "Good ivy," goes an old carol, "say to us what birds hast thou."

The owl is often used as a symbol in the logos of academic institutions and organizations. The owl, with its alert but stern countenance, seems to exude intelligence. We marvel at the night predator that on silent wings brings quick death to its hapless prey.

As the symbolism of the owl is mixed, so too are the perceptions we have concerning them. Myra Cohn Livingston, in a book of poems about owls, *If the Owl Calls Again*, selected a variety of poems that show the whole spectrum of people's feelings about owls.[2] Leonard Clark sees owls as "ugly phantoms of the night" and states, "I do not like owls."[3] John Haines writes of his longings to fly and hunt with the owl.[4] Randall Jarrell speaks of the fear owls engender in their potential prey:

The Bird of Night

> A shadow is floating through the moonlight.
> Its wings don't make a sound.
> Its claws are long, its beak is bright.
> Its eyes try all the corners of the night.
>
> It calls and calls: all the air swells and heaves
> And washes up and down like water.
> The ear that listens to the owl believes
> In death. The bat beneath the eaves.

> The mice beside the stone are still as death—
> The owl's air washes them like water.
> The owl goes back and forth inside the night,
> And the night holds its breath.[5]

In ancient Indian folklore the owl stands for wisdom and helpfulness and has the power of prophecy. The same theme is stated in Aesop's fables. In the Middle Ages, the owl's persona was altered when, as a night bird, it was associated with witches and evildoers and thus became a symbol of evil and dread. During the Middle Ages, the owl came to represent Jews, considered by many Christians to live in spiritual darkness.

In some parts of the world the message of the owl can supposedly be discerned from the number of its hoots or screeches. In southern India, the following formula applied:

1 screech	=	death
2 screeches	=	success in an undertaking
3 screeches	=	arrival, by marriage, of a girl in the family
4 screeches	=	a disturbance
5 screeches	=	travel by the hearer
6 screeches	=	guests are coming
7 screeches	=	mental distress
8 screeches	=	sudden death
9 screeches	=	favorable results

In Illinois, one owl "holler" meant that one person was about to rob you; two "hollers" meant that two people would do the job. To the Asinai Native American tribe, an owl was such a friend that, no matter how many hoots, the sound of an owl was cause for great joy.

The owl has been thought in many cultures and in many times to be a prognosticator of weather. An early indication of the owl's supposed prowess in this area comes from about 300 years B.C., from the Greek Theophrastus, who said that an owl hooting quietly in a storm denotes fair weather; likewise if it hoots quietly on a winter's night. In Brittany, an owl hooting in the evening meant good weather for the next day. In France, an owl hooting in a rainstorm meant that good weather was on the way. The Native American Pawnee, Omaha, and Osage tribes thought the owl to be a fair-weather prophet. Screeching owls foretold bad weather in parts of Ontario and Newfoundland and hailstorms in England.

Thus, we are left to assign whatever values we want to owls. In folklore history they have been both hero and villain, scourge and boon, hailed and dreaded. Whatever owls have been, they have never been ignored.

DISCUSSION

Description

The northern spotted owl (*Strix occidentalis caurina*) stands between 14 inches (36 centimeters) and 2 feet (60 centimeters) tall and weighs up to about 22 ounces (625 grams). It has chocolate-colored plumage dappled with white spots. Its eyes seem very large for its body and stand out like two great onyx cabochons. The northern spotted owl is one of three spotted owl subspecies, the others being the California spotted owl and the Mexican spotted owl.

Habitat

Northern spotted owls live primarily in old-growth and mature forests. There a high canopy covers the forest and large, overstory trees predominate. There is some open space for flying and an accumulation of fallen trees leaves woody debris on the ground. Also available in this habitat are snags and broken trees that afford cavities for nesting and perching and support for the owls' prey. The owl can live in a younger forest if all these conditions exist. Most remaining northern spotted owl habitat is on public land managed by the U.S. Forest Service, Bureau of Land Management, or the National Park Service.

Historic Range and Current Distribution

There are no reliable estimates concerning the historic range of the northern spotted owl, but this bird is believed to have lived in most older forests throughout the Pacific Northwest, before modern settlement reduced the area available for nesting. Most of these former forest lands have been cleared for settlement or through the harvesting of timber.

The northern spotted owl is found from southwestern British Columbia, Canada, through western Washington, western Oregon, and the Coast Range area of northwestern California south to San Francisco Bay (see fig. 8.1, page 104). Approximately 2,000 breeding pairs have been located, although the present population is believed to number between 3,000 and 5,000 pairs. One estimate says that this number of pairs represents about one-half the number that existed in 1800. Further, the slow breeding rate of the bird suggests that it would take a century for the number to return to its size of two centuries ago.

Reasons for Endangerment and Attempts to Help

The decline of the northern spotted owl has been associated with the loss of habitat due to cutting of old-growth timber. The conservation of the northern spotted owl is controversial because it is intertwined with the management of old-growth forests in the Northwest. In January of 1987, the U.S. Fish and Wildlife Service was petitioned by Greenworld to list the northern spotted owl as endangered. In August of the same year, another petition was received from the Sierra Club Legal Defense Fund, Inc., on behalf of nearly thirty conservation organizations. The Service found that the listing was not warranted at the time, but this ruling was challenged in court and the court ruled against the Service. The northern spotted owl was listed as threatened on June 23, 1989. The listing has had an enormous impact on the logging industry. The northern spotted owl became endangered because of loss of habitat, but the harvesting of old-growth forests has been a policy of logging interests for at least the last century, and so the owl's listing has pitted conservationists against the logging industry, with the specter of unemployment looming as the price for saving the owl.

The conservation strategy currently proposed is unprecedented. A network of "habitat conservation areas" would be preserved throughout the owl's range, each large enough to support a minimum of twenty owl pairs. The areas would be located within twelve miles of each other. The plan seems to be a compromise between owl conservation and industry interests. Not all the habitat of the northern spotted owl would be saved, but there would be enough so that the owl could probably survive the next hundred years.

Fig. 8.1. Present and historic range of the northern spotted owl.

The Bureau of Land Management (BLM) will develop its own management strategy aimed at conserving the owl on its lands while continuing high timber harvest levels. The BLM will investigate whether such measures as supplemental feeding, setting out nesting boxes, and captive breeding of owls for release can counterbalance the loss of owl habitat.

NORTHERN SPOTTED OWL ACTIVITIES

Northern Spotted Owl and the Environment

- Read the article by Ted Gup, "Owl vs. Man," from the June 25, 1990 issue of *Time* (see bibliography). This article clearly delineates the controversy surrounding the northern spotted owl. At issue is a conflict between environmentalists and the logging industry. An article by Michael Satchell, "The Endangered Logger," in the June 25, 1990 *U.S. News & World Report* gives the loggers' side of the story. Plan and participate in a discussion featuring both the loggers' and the environmentalists' points of view.

- In figure 8.2 the article titled "Cost Data Hiked on Spotted Owl" estimates that 40,000 jobs in timbering and related industries will be lost by 1995. Figure out what related industries are affected. Make a web (fig. 8.3, page 106) showing these jobs.

Cost data hiked on spotted owl

WASHINGTON — The government's proposal to protect the northern spotted owl would cost the Pacific Northwest about 40,000 jobs in timbering and related industries by 1995, roughly three jobs out of every four expected to exist otherwise, Fish and Wildlife Service economists said. The estimated loss would be 57 percent more than what was projected under earlier planned restrictions on logging.

Fig. 8.2. *The Denver Post* (April 30, 1991). Reprinted with the permission of *The Denver Post*.

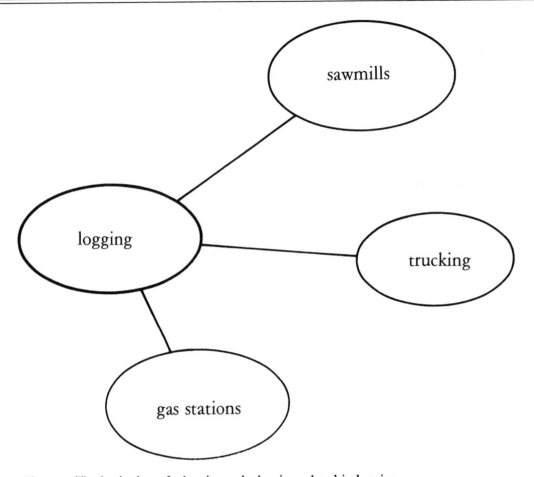

Fig. 8.3. The beginning of a logging web showing related industries.

- In figure 8.4 the article titled "Spotted Owl Found Nailed to Sign; Note Threatens Fire" gives an alarming reaction to the spotted owl controversy. Stage a meeting in which a more acceptable protest is suggested.

- Write or call:

     Bureau of Land Management
     P.O. Box 2965
     Portland, OR 97208
     Phone: (503) 280-7027

  requesting the latest information on conservation plans concerning the northern spotted owl. Read enough to know the arguments on both sides of this controversy. Form your own opinion about the issue. Write your congressperson and your senators to let them know your opinion and the legislation you would like to see adopted regarding the spotted owl.

- Design an assembly program for your school to call attention to the plight of the northern spotted owl. Contact the Raptor Society or other conservation group and ask a handler to bring an owl to your school.

Spotted owl found nailed to sign; note threatens fire

Associated Press

PORT ANGELES, Wash. — A dead spotted owl found nailed to a sign in Olympic National Park bore a note warning "the match has yet to be struck" in the battle over old-growth forests.

Acting chief ranger Curt Sauer pulled the young owl off the nail and found a typewritten note tucked under a fold of broken skin. A wooden match stuck straight out from the bird's ruffled breast feathers.

"If you think your parks and wilderness don't have enough of these suckers, plant this one," the note read. "They talk of social unrest. The match has yet to be struck."

Sauer, who found the bird Monday along Hurricane Ridge Road, said he believed the match reference was a threat of forest fires in the park.

The U.S. Fish and Wildlife Service planned a necropsy on the owl.

Sauer said a "substantial" reward would be offered for information leading to conviction of the person responsible for killing the bird. No amount was specified.

Because the Fish and Wildlife Service declared the owl to be a threatened species last summer under the Endangered Species Act, killing one is a federal crime. The maximum penalty is a year in jail and a $100,000 fine.

Park officials said they were not concerned about the fire threat in midwinter with snow and rain dampening the forests.

A panel of government scientists led by U.S. Forest Service biologist Jack Ward Thomas warned last April the owl was on the road to extinction because its habitat was being cut down. The owl lives primarily in the old-growth forests of the Northwest.

Thomas warned logging would need to be curtailed on 3 million acres of Northwest forests to save the bird. Most of the old-growth timber is found in national forests managed by the U.S. Forest Service. Various studies estimated thousands of forest industry jobs would be lost under such a logging curtailment.

No logging is permitted in national parks.

Jerry Leppell, president of the Loggers Solidarity Committee in the Olympic Peninsula town of Forks, said the owl killing was "not the right thing to do, but just try to tell that to a person who just lost everything he worked for."

Leppell said he does not know of any specific plans to set fires in the park but added, "I've heard rumors."

Tim Cullinan of the Olympic Peninsula Audubon Society said, "We had hoped it wouldn't happen but I guess it doesn't surprise me that it has. Obviously there are extremists on both sides of this debate."

Three years ago, two young owls were found dead, apparently clubbed to death in the Hood Canal Ranger District in Olympic National Park.

Leppell said that until the government realizes what economic hardship it is causing in the timber towns and remedies the situation, "you're going to have the worst nightmare you've ever seen — from both sides."

Despite numerous hearings, Congress ended 1990 without passing any legislation to deal with the owl dilemma.

Fig. 8.4. *Rocky Mountain News* (January 20, 1991): 206. Reprinted with permission of the *Rocky Mountain News*.

- Prepare a map showing the current habitat area of the northern spotted owl.

- A conservation plan for the northern spotted owl calls for setting aside 2,200 acres of old-growth forest for each nesting pair. If there are 3,000 nesting pairs of northern spotted owls, how many acres must be saved?

- There is considerable controversy over how much range a pair of nesting northern spotted owls needs. The birds seem to adjust to the amount of space available. In Oregon, where space is more limited, pairs seem to range over about 2,500 acres. In Washington, where more space is available, they range over about 10,000 acres. Rework the formula mentioned in the previous activity (2,200 acres per nesting pair), substituting 10,000 acres per nesting pair, and compare the results.

• In figure 8.5 the article titled "Concern for Endangered Owl Is Stalling Cancer Research" links a cancer treatment with the yew tree that is within the spotted owl's environment. In small groups, make a list of the pros and cons for protecting the spotted owl and its environment and prioritize the list. Compare the lists and discuss the similarities and differences.

Concern for endangered owl is stalling cancer research

Scientists need trees as a source of drug for clinical testing

Associated Press

GRANTS PASS, Ore. — The battle against cancer is about to collide with the drive to protect the habitat of the northern spotted owl, the focus of a dispute about use of the Northwest's oldest forests.

The National Cancer Institute wants 720,000 pounds of bark harvested from the Pacific yew this year to produce 55 pounds of a compound called taxol for intensive clinical testing as an anticancer drug.

But harvesting that much bark would mean intrusions into forests set aside as sanctuaries for the northern spotted owl, which was listed as a threatened species last year.

Closing those forests has undercut the Northwest's powerful timber industry.

Taxol has shown promise against ovarian cancer, which claims 12,000 victims a year. It also is being tested against breast, lung and colon cancers, said Saul Schepartz, a biochemist in the National Cancer Institute's therapeutics development program.

Until now, foresters have treated the Pacific yew as a weed.

No other natural source of taxol has been found.

But the Florida State Office of Research, on behalf of professor Robert Holton, has filed U.S. and foreign patent applications for a process that can produce taxol without the bark.

Holton's process joins two chemicals to form the drug. One of

those chemicals can be synthesized easily in the laboratory, he says. The other is more complex, but a team of French scientists recently found that it can be extracted from the leaves of the English yew.

Harvesting yews at a rate of 36,000 trees a year from an inventory of 1.2 million mature trees would put heavy pressure on the species, which takes 200 years to grow to a trunk diameter of 12 inches.

"If we do that, we will kill the goose that laid the golden egg," said Jerry Rust, a Lane County commissioner who is active in the Native Yew Conservation Committee.

Fig. 8.5. *Rocky Mountain News* (January 25, 1991): 45. Reprinted with permission of the *Rocky Mountain News*.

Northern Spotted Owl and the Arts

• Make a mask of the northern spotted owl from the plans in figure 8.6, pages 109-14.

Directions for Making an Owl Mask

The mask or hood pattern shown in this figure measures only about 7 inches by 10.5 inches. The actual size of the pattern should be about 11 inches by 17 inches. You can enlarge these pages in one of two ways. First, you can copy the page from this book and take it to a commercial print shop and have it enlarged to 11 inches by 17 inches (folio size). Another way is to use an opaque projector. Project the image on a sheet of tagboard or construction material, adjust the size of the image until it is 11 inches by 17 inches, and then trace the image. There are two sides to the mask design, printed here as front and back. Once you have your mask pattern at the required size, follow the directions here.

1. Cut out all the mask pieces along the dotted lines.

2. Use the feather pattern to cut out approximately 60 to 70 pieces per mask.

3. Use photographs of owls for ideas to decorate the mask pieces to give them more realistic markings.

4. Glue the headband strip to the face part of the head-piece where indicated by the "x"s on the back of the face piece.

5. Fold over the center strap and adjust to fit to child's head. Glue to the center back of the headband.

6. Attach the first row of feather pieces, over-lapping the sides of each slightly. Glue along the sides of the center strap first, then along the headband piece. Work one side, then the other.

7. Add two to three more rows of feathers to the headband from the inside, again over-lapping the pieces' sides slightly.

(Fig. 8.6 continues on page 110.)

Fig. 8.6. The owl mask (directions and patterns).

Fig. 8.6. — *Continued*

8. Gently curve the feathers inward towards the center strap and glue underneath the headpiece feathers. Fill in any open spaces with feathers attached from the inside.

9. Add a row of feathers down the center strap of the headpiece and along the bottom half of the headband strap to give the mask a more finished look.

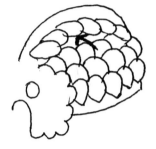

10. Attach the face piece to the headpiece by gluing just around the eyes and nose cutouts where indicated. Line up the two parts and press together at the "x"s.

11. Fold the beak in half along the solid line. To glue the beak, place glue along the inside curve and press together at the "x"s.

12. Fold in the tabs on the beak. Apply glue to the tabs and sides of the beak where indicated. Line up between the eyes and attach to the "x"s.

Options: Instead of cutting the feather shapes, tear the paper into the approximate shape. Dip the ends of the feathers into poster paint before applying to give the mask an overall spotted look.

(Photograph courtesy
of Deborah McGlathery.)

Fig. 8.6. — *Continued*

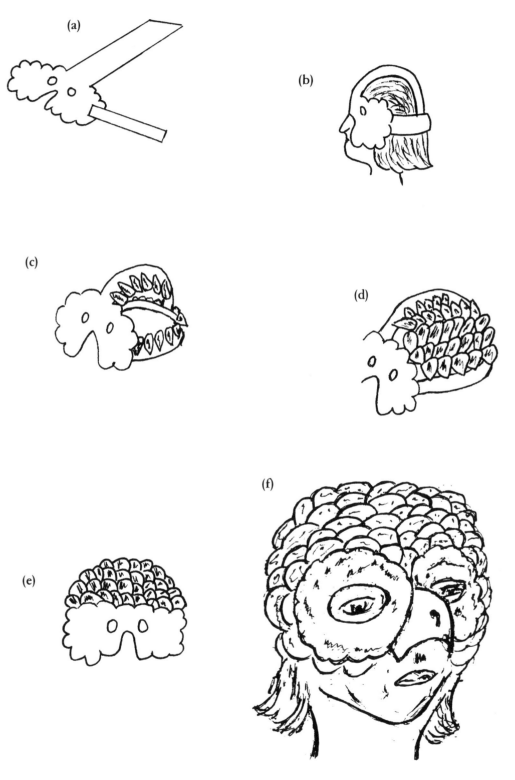

(a)

(b)

(c)

(d)

(f)

(e)

(Fig. 8.6 continues on page 112.)

Fig. 8.6. — *Continued*

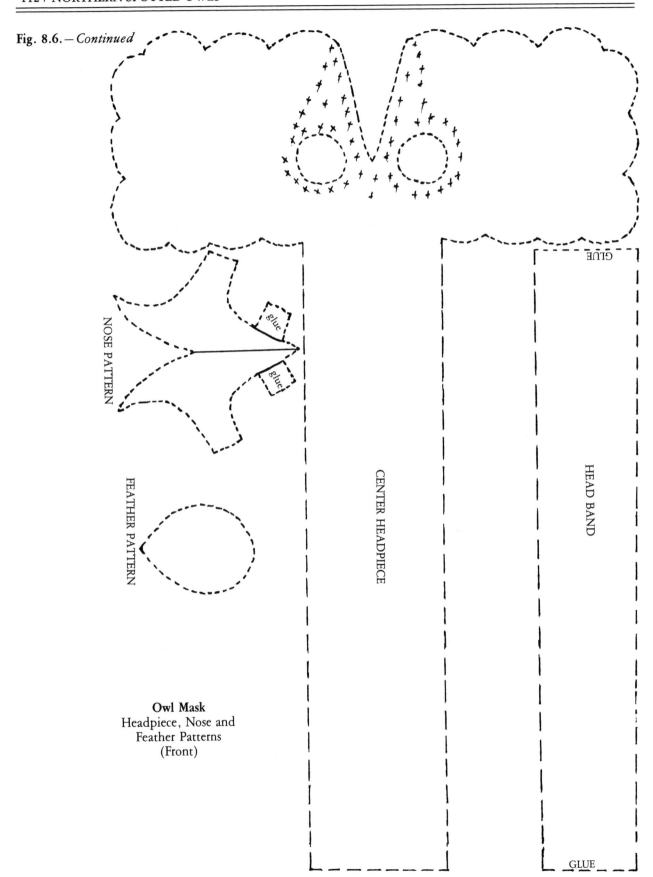

NOSE PATTERN

FEATHER PATTERN

CENTER HEADPIECE

HEAD BAND

GLUE

GLUE

glue

glue

Owl Mask
Headpiece, Nose and
Feather Patterns
(Front)

Fig. 8.6. — *Continued*

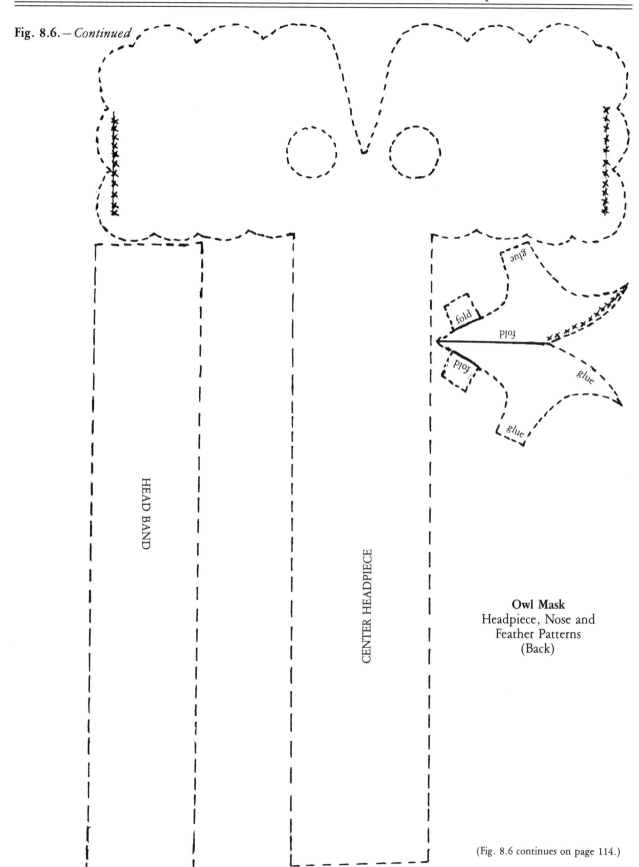

HEAD BAND

CENTER HEADPIECE

Owl Mask
Headpiece, Nose and
Feather Patterns
(Back)

(Fig. 8.6 continues on page 114.)

Fig. 8.6. — *Continued*

Owl Mask
Face Piece Pattern
(Front)

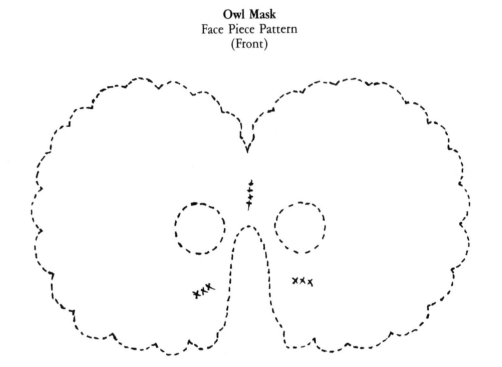

Owl Mask
Face Piece Pattern
(Back)

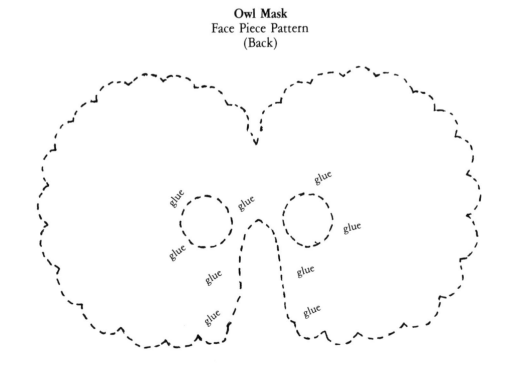

- Write and produce a play starring the northern spotted owl. Have as characters at least a pair of owls with their two offspring. Have them discuss the onslaught of logging and the effect it has on them. Use the masks you made in the previous activity.

- Some of the same problems that changed the value of cotton in the South within the last century—land mismanagement and politics—seem to be paralleled in the spotted-owl-versus-logging-industry controversy. People of the South have recovered from the devastating decline of cotton production as the "king" industry and now are part of a stronger, more diversified economy. In Enterprise, Alabama, citizens have even built a monument to the boll weevil, an insect largely responsible for the demise of the great cotton industry. One member of the logging industry suggested that one day citizens of the Northwest might erect a monument to the northern spotted owl. Design such a monument and compose the words to put on the monument's plaque.

- Review the folklore of the owl and the folklore of the wolf. You will notice that both have been associated with evil. Write a dialogue between a wolf and an owl about what they consider misunderstandings about their characters. If you want to stage this dialogue as a play, use the owl mask you can make from figure 8.6 on pages 109-14 and the wolf mask you can make from figure 2.1, pages 20-22.

- Design a shoebox-size diorama depicting the northern spotted owl in its habitat.

- Make a collection of newspaper stories about the northern spotted owl. Design a bulletin board featuring these clippings.

- Design a bumper sticker that states your feelings about the northern spotted owl. Organize a contest in your classroom or in your school and display the results.

Northern Spotted Owl and Literature

- Write a series of haiku-form poems about the northern spotted owl. Remember that the haiku form has three lines. There are five syllables in the first line, seven syllables in the second line, and five syllables in the third line. The lines do not normally rhyme.

- Look at a copy of Paul Fleischman's *Joyful Noise: Poems for Two Voices* to see a poem form you might want to try. Compose a poem to be read by two voices in Fleischman's style.

- There is a lot of folklore information about owls. Become familiar with some of it (from reading the folklore section of this chapter or from other sources) and then make up your own myths and legends about owls; for example, how the owl can turn its head almost in a complete circle; why the owl looks like a cat, etc.

NOTES

1. John Keats, "The Eve of St. Agnes," in *Selected Poems and Letters*, ed. Douglas Bush (Boston: Houghton Mifflin, 1959).

2. Myra Cohn Livingston, *If the Owl Calls Again: A Collection of Owl Poems* (New York: Margaret K. McElderry, 1990).

3. Leonard Clark, in *If the Owl Calls Again*, 101.

4. John Haines, in *If the Owl Calls Again*, 41.

5. John Haines, in *If the Owl Calls Again*, 32. Reprinted with permission of Macmillan Publishing Company from THE BAT-POET by Randall Jarrell. Copyright © Macmillan Publishing Company, 1963, 1964.

RESOURCE BIBLIOGRAPHY

Books

Campbell, Robert Wayne, E. D. Forsman, and B. M. Van Der Raay. *An Annotated Bibliography of Literature on the Spotted Owl*. Victoria, B.C.: Province of British Columbia, Ministry of Forests, 1984.
A report on land management and an extensive spotted owl bibliography.

Fleischman, Paul. *Joyful Noise: Poems for Two Voices*. New York: Harper & Row, 1988.
This exceptional volume of poetry features the insect rather than the owl, but serves as a form for a suggested activity included in this chapter. The poems are to be read aloud by two people. Exciting illustrations by Eric Meadows complement the text, which is a unique guide to the insect world that captures the sights and sounds of the phylum.

Harris, Lorle K., ed. *Tlingit Tales: Potlatch and Totem Pole*. Happy Camp, Calif.: Naturegraph Publishers, 1985.
Legends of the Tlingit people are retold by Robert Zuboff, head of the Beaver Clan. Among them are "How the Owl Came to Be."

Krutch, Joseph Word, comp. *The World of Animals: A Treasury of Lore, Legend, and Literature by Great Writers and Naturalists from the 5th Century B.C. to the Present*. New York: Simon and Schuster, 1961.
"Noted scholars and gifted amateurs" write about a variety of animals. Some well-known naturalists—Audubon, Darwin, and others—are represented, as well as literary giants such as Twain, Melville, Dickens, and Steinbeck. Mr. Krutch provides cogent and sensitive commentary as an accompaniment to the selections.

Livingston, Myra Cohn. *If the Owl Calls Again: A Collection of Owl Poems*. New York: Margaret K. McElderry, 1990.
Ms. Livingston has collected a varied selection of poems that deal with owls. Some show the dark side of owls, some show the light side, but all are interesting and help us understand our fascination with this bird. The accompanying woodcuts by Antonio Frasconi are exceptional.

Weinstein, Krystyna. *Owls, Owls, Fantastical Fowls*. New York: Arch Publishing, 1985.
Ms. Weinstein shows how the owl has been depicted throughout history in art, legend, literature, and folktales. She describes the place of owls in the lore of dozens of cultures, showing that owls have been portrayed as evil omens as well as harbingers of happiness. This is as complete a literary history of owls as one can imagine.

Yolen, Jane. *Owl Moon*. New York: Philomel Books, 1987.
> This delightfully told and beautifully illustrated story of a boy walking with his father on a winter evening to see the great horned owl will capture the hearts of children and adults alike.

Yolen, Jane, ed. *Favorite Folktales from Around the World*. New York: Pantheon Books, 1986.
> This compilation features favorite stories from over forty cultures, interestingly told and thoughtfully grouped by theme. Each chapter, a group of tales of the same ilk, is beautifully introduced by the editor. A short treatise on the story and the storyteller serves as an introduction to the book.

Magazine Articles

"Environment's Little Big Bird." *Time* 135 (April 16, 1990): 21.
> This short news article reports on the status of the efforts to save the spotted owl and the ancient forests in which it lives.

Gup, Ted. "Owl vs. Man." *Time* 135 (June 25, 1990): 56-62.
> This article clearly delineates the issues in the controversy of which the northern spotted owl is the central figure. Excellent graphics and statistical information give the reader the bases for the arguments on each side of the conflict between environmentalists and the logging industry.

"How Many Owls Is Too Many Owls?" *Mother Earth News* 121 (January/February 1990): 26.
> This article reports on a bill adopted by Congress in October of 1989 that provides for a slight reduction in the amount of old-growth cutting on federal lands in Oregon and Washington. The bill is an attempt to protect spotted owl habitat in the national forests "as much as possible."

Line, Les. "Gambits and Skirmishes." *Audubon* 92 (May 1990): 4.
> The editor of *Audubon* gives a progress report on the battle to save ancient forests and the tiny owls that live there.

"No Peace for the Owl." *Time* 136 (July 9, 1990): 63.
> This brief article looks at the apparent contradiction in President Bush's announcement of a plan to save the spotted owl, the forests where it lives, and loggers' jobs, all at the same time.

Satchell, Michael. "The Endangered Logger." *U.S. News & World Report* 108 (June 25, 1990): 27-29.
> The author gives data illustrating the logging industry's side of the controversy surrounding the northern spotted owl's placement on the endangered species list.

Bald Eagles

KING OF THE SKY

Based on a Cherokee Story

A long time ago, even before the coming of the white people, even before the proud Cherokee walked on the earth, the birds were in constant argument about which of them could fly the highest. Some claimed that they could win any contest. Others, certain that they could not complete with their high-flying relatives, simply sat around and discussed it.

"Surely the vulture can fly the highest," argued the blue jay in his loud, cracking voice. "I watch him soar into the sky with no effort. He circles higher and higher until even my fine eyes can see him only as a speck. I imagine he can fly so high that he is closer to the sun than to the earth."

"That may be," chimed in the magpie, "but I doubt seriously that he can beat my friend the hawk. Hawk is the very spirit of fight. He can fly fast, true, and straight. He can also fly very high. Even I, and I am a very good flier," the magpie modestly continued, "cannot begin to keep up with my cousin the hawk. I would certainly vote for him."

"The eagle," shrieked the crow, "could beat either one of them. Eagle flies high in fair weather or foul. While we fly for shelter in the great northern storms, Eagle flies into the thunderheads and makes play of the strong winds, lightning, and rain. The eagle is the king of the sky."

"Don't be too sure," chirped the proud little cowbird. "I could beat all of the birds you think are such great, high fliers. You almost never get above the treetops, but I, I can fly so high that I look the sun straight in the eye. I could beat all of those you have named and all of the ones you haven't." A tiny, sly smile parted his beak.

All the birds in hearing distance laughed loudly at the tiny cowbird, but Cowbird did not back down. He kept his cunning smile as the other birds mocked him. Finally he said, "Let's go to Owl and see if he can help us settle this argument."

The birds gathered around the wise old owl and noisily presented their various arguments. The owl listened patiently, though the chirps, squawks, caws, and other sounds became almost a roar as each bird loudly argued for a favorite. Finally the old owl shushed the other birds and they all leaned forward as Owl began to speak.

"I have heard your arguments," he began, "and they all have some merit. I don't know what difference it makes, but if you like I'll judge a contest for all willing birds and we can settle this argument that has been raging for so long."

Owl asked the vulture, eagle, and hawk if they would participate. Each said that he would.

"Then the contest will be tomorrow and I will judge. My decision will be final. We have the strong contenders here, but to make it fair, if there are any others among you wanting to fly tomorrow, let it be known."

The other birds shook their heads slowly, knowing that they would only be embarrassed in the competition. Cowbird, however, held his head high and chirped that he would like to be a contestant. The other birds stared in disbelief, but the owl reminded them that the contest was open to all. The birds stayed up very late that night discussing who might be named king of the sky. The endless arguments did not change anyone's opinion, but the birds were almost unanimous in ridiculing the cowbird for even being in the contest.

Morning finally came and all the birds gathered to watch the start of the event. The contestants were all there except the cowbird.

"Just as I suspected," cawed the crow. "That silly cowbird doesn't have the nerve to show his face here."

The owl started the race and the contestants began to climb. Hawk was first off, flying fast and straight as an arrow toward the brilliant morning sun. The vulture's start seemed to require a lot of effort. He flapped heavily as he sought to gain altitude. His supporters were not surprised. They knew that Vulture was a slow and awkward starter, but he became more majestic as he rose and began to circle, riding the thermals of the morning air. Eagle, too, was a pretty slow starter, but quickly passed the vulture and soon was much higher. Spectators strained their eyes to see what was happening. Owl, with his very keen eyes, kept them informed.

"Eagle is the highest by far," reported Owl. "Hawk has turned back and given up the race. Vulture, too, seems ready to concede to Eagle. Eagle seems to be the winner."

All the birds began to cheer. "Hooray for Eagle! King of the Sky!"

"Wait," interrupted Owl. "I see something on Eagle's back. It's ... it's Cowbird! He has been hiding in Eagle's feathers!" As Eagle began his return, Cowbird fluttered up a little higher before beginning his long journey back.

"Not fair," chirped most of the birds in disbelief.

As the contestants came back to where Owl sat, Cowbird began to boast about his victory. "See? What did I tell you? I flew higher than Hawk, or Vulture, or Eagle. I am King of the Sky!"

All the birds looked at Owl to see what he might say.

"I told you that I would judge the contest," began the wise old bird, "and now I am ready to announce who is King of the Sky."

Cowbird stood as tall as he could, with his little chest puffed out as large as he could make it, and waited for his name to be called. All the birds looked straight at Owl and listened hard for what he might say.

"Eagle is King of the Sky," pronounced Owl.

The birds cheered at the decision, all except Cowbird, who went into a pout.

Owl continued, "Eagle must be declared King of the Sky, for he not only flew the highest of the contestants, he did it with the added weight of this sly little cowbird. There is no doubt. Eagle is the winner."

From that day on, the birds never again argued over who could fly the highest. Oh, they did spend a lot of time discussing the great race—the strength of the contestants and the cunning of Cowbird—but each knew for certain that a great champion had been crowned and that Eagle would forever be known as King of the Sky.

FOLKLORE

The eagle appears in the folklore of many cultures. The eagle in profile was one of the symbols in ancient Egyptian hieroglyphics. In the religion of the Egyptians, the eagle represented the soaring soul of man, humankind. When the Phoenicians changed hieroglypics to an alphabet, the eagle symbol became the basis for the lowercase *a* (see fig. 9.1).

Fig. 9.1.

The eagle was sacred to the ancient sky gods of Greece and Rome, Zeus and Jupiter.

Eagles wintered in the lower Euphrates Valley and were venerated by the Sumerians. The eagle is a chief character in the Sumerian myth of Ethana. In this myth, an eagle, in the process of stealing eggs, was attacked by a large snake, which was killed by a peasant named Ethana. In gratitude, the eagle carried Ethana on a trip to the heavens, but she was rejected by the gods and fell back to earth. The legend illustrates an early concept of the human spirit ascending to heaven. The pitting of an eagle against a snake has been used as a theme of European artists for centuries.

The eagle was the totem of the Caesars of the Roman Empire and was thought to carry imperial souls to heaven. The funeral of Augustus Caesar featured this motif in an interesting fashion. The body of the dead emperor was carried on an ivory bier to a pyramid-shaped funeral pyre. An eagle that was concealed in the top of the pyramid was released at a designated point in the ritual to symbolize the emperor's soul ascending to heaven.

Charlemagne used the eagle as a motif on helmets and shields. The eagle was also used as the symbol of John the Evangelist in the Middle Ages. Later Germanic emperors of the Holy Roman Empire adopted the eagle of the Caesars and it eventually became the heraldic symbol of many of the royal families of Europe.

The eagle is associated with all sorts of sky and weather phenomena. It was said to cause lightning and fire and to make the winds blow when it shook its wings. The eagle was thought to be able to look straight at the sun and gather great strength from it.

In Germanic and Norse tradition, the eagle is a gloomy giant. Eagles are also connected to cultural heroes and tricksters, often as victims, or appear as the powerful totems of heroes. The eagle is a rescuer, a source of strength and magical power, the animal form assumed by the hero and, sometimes, an egotistical character.

Seeing an eagle from a high place, such as a church steeple or high mountain, means high honors. Owning an eagle is good luck and brings strength and power. Eating the raw heart of a male eagle brings bravery and strength. Wearing a tuft of eagle feathers in one's hat gives the wearer the eagle's sight and courage. Seeing an eagle rise from the ground and soar indicates overcoming personal difficulties. Seeing an eagle with a snake in its claws is a good omen. An eagle can keep one safe from lightning.

To some Native American peoples, the golden eagle is the primary messenger of the Great Spirit. It is the most direct connection to the Creator. The eagle comes to the Native American tribes in many forms and spirits. In one form, it represents the Thunderbird Spirit, who brings the rain and storms. Eagle feathers are the most honorable prizes for the warrior.

According to ancient legend, the Aztecs found their promised land in a valley in Mexico. There, as had been foretold, they saw a great eagle on a cactus plant with a snake in its talons. The golden eagle of the legend was adopted as the symbol of the Republic of Mexico in 1821 and is pictured on the silver peso, one of Mexico's coins. American artists used the eagle-snake relationship as an allegorical reference to what enemies of the United States could expect.

The bald eagle was chosen as the symbol of the United States of America in 1789. The eagle is used in the symbols and logos of many different organizations; for example, it is in the logo of the United States Postal Service and is prominent on the Congressional Medal of Honor. It is in the Eagle Scout badge of the Boy Scouts of America and was the symbol of Apollo 11, the mission that achieved the first lunar landing. George Washington's jacket buttons were decorated with eagles. The eagle has similarly graced the sterns of warships, faces of public buildings, coins, bank notes, furniture, and quilts.

DISCUSSION

Description

The bald eagle (*Haliaeetus leucocephalus*) is a large bird of prey, or raptor. Its body measures 32 to 40 inches (80 to 100 centimeters) long. The wingspan may reach 7.5 feet (2.3 meters). Adult birds range in color from dark brown to black, with white head and tail and yellow beak and feet. Immature bald eagles, with their dark brown bodies and mottled white wings, are often mistaken for golden eagles. The distinctive white markings do not appear until the fourth year.

Behavior

The bald eagle feeds primarily on fish, but will also eat rodents and other small mammals. It will also compete with vultures for carrion. Characteristically, the bald eagle circles when hunting, scanning the ground with its keen eyes. It dives suddenly to catch its prey, sinking its formidable talons into the flesh and flying away with its catch. Although named as the national bird in 1782 for what seemed an independent and fierce demeanor, the bald eagle is actually quite shy.

Bald eagles are thought to mate for life. They engage in spectacular courting rituals that include high-speed diving and somersaults. Mating birds often lock talons in mid-air. After mating, the birds construct a nest in a tall tree or on the side of a cliff. The nest, among the largest constructed by birds, is made of sticks and foliage and is lined with finer material such as down. Because nests are used and added to year after year, they can grow to be very large. A nest discovered in Ohio in the nineteenth century measured 12 feet (3.7 meters) deep and 9 feet (2.7 meters) in diameter.[1]

Females generally lay two eggs between October and March, depending on the latitude of the breeding area. Both birds sit on the eggs over a thirty-five-day incubation period. The chicks, which are covered with white downy feathers, are fed for about three months, by which time they are able to fly. The adults then drive the young away to hunt on their own.

Most bald eagles migrate south in the fall, so that thousands can be sighted in the lower forty-eight states during November through March. The National Wildlife Federation reported in 1988 that there were 11,241 wintering bald eagles throughout these lower states, mostly in the west and midwest. At night flocks of these wintering birds gather in trees that, like their summer nests, are used year after year.

Habitat

Eagles generally nest in mature forests, particularly in conifers such as ponderosa and loblolly pines. They prefer areas where there is a flowing stream or open water and plenty of fish.

Historic Range and Current Distribution

Bald eagles once nested in at least forty-five of the forty-eight lower states, Canada, and Alaska (see fig. 9.2, page 124). Their decline began in the nineteenth century and accelerated in the 1940s.

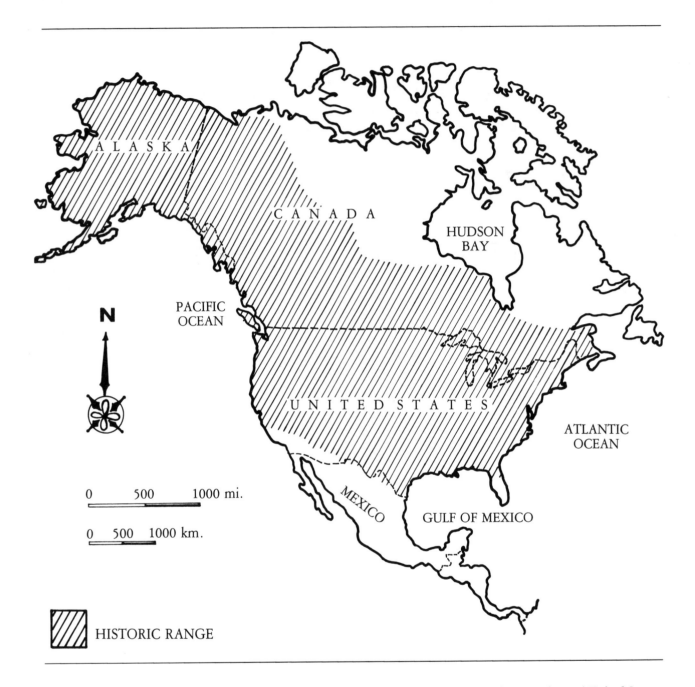

Fig. 9.2. Historic nesting areas of the bald eagle included Canada, Alaska, and most of the continental United States.

Most of the breeding pairs of bald eagles are in Alaska; some 30,000 individuals are in that population. The western provinces of Canada are home to another large population. According to the Fish and Wildlife Service, the lower 48 states hosted 2,440 breeding pairs in 1988, with the greatest numbers found in the Pacific Northwest, the upper Great Lakes, Florida, and around the Chesapeake Bay area. A large concentration, 305 pairs, is found in Washington State on the San Juan Islands and the Olympic Peninsula coastline (see fig. 9.3).

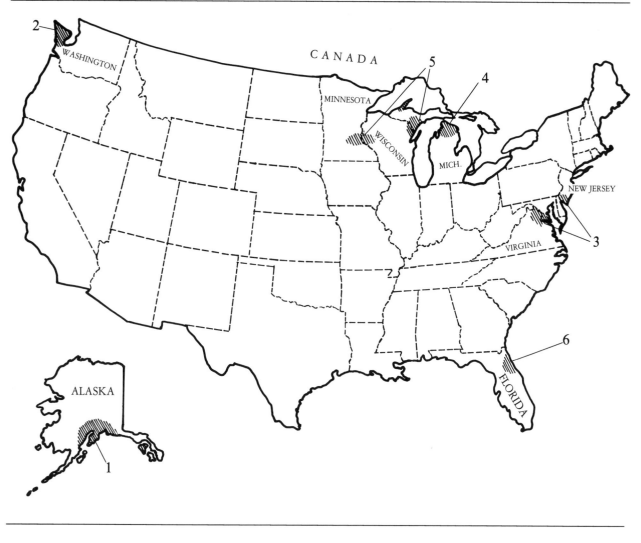

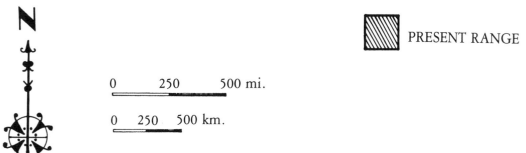

Fig. 9.3. Present range of the bald eagle: 1. Alaska; 2. Washington State; 3. Around the Chesapeake Bay area; 4. Michigan; 5. Upper Great Lakes, including Minnesota and Wisconsin; 6. Florida; and in smaller numbers throughout the United States and Canada.

One thousand eleven pairs nested in 1988 in the Northern and Great Plains states, principally in Minnesota, Wisconsin, and Michigan. In the southeast, 531 pairs nest in Florida. The Chesapeake Bay area houses 181 pairs nested in Maryland, Delaware, and Virginia.

Reasons for Decline and Attempts to Help

The bald eagle population began to decline in the 1940s because of hunting, habitat alteration, and human encroachment. The most severe impact came from the introduction of the pesticide DDT (dichlorodiphenyltrichloroethane). Residues of this pesticide were carried up the food chain and concentrated in the tissues of large predators such as eagles. The toxic effect of the DDT made eagle eggshells too thin to bear the weight of the incubating parents, so many eggs were destroyed in the nest. The crash in population was abrupt and dramatic. By 1981, active nests were known to exist in only thirty states and about 90 percent of the pairs were concentrated in just ten states. The Chesapeake Bay population fell from 150 pairs in 1962 to about 85 pairs in 1970. Nesters, once common along the Atlantic seaboard from the Chesapeake Bay to the Florida Keys, retreated until in the late 1970s only the Florida population was secure.

The ban of DDT in the United States had an immediate effect on the eagle population. The population began to improve, while recovery was aided by federal efforts that included monitoring, improved protection, captive breeding, relocation, and excellent publicity. By 1981, the nesting population in the lower forty-eight states had doubled. The recovery has been so dramatic that the Fish and Wildlife Service is in the process of reclassifying part of the bald eagle populations in the lower states from endangered to threatened. Relocation—the release of chicks taken from nests in Alaska in states with few nesting pairs—has been so successful that the Fish and Wildlife Service has been able to discontinue its captive breeding program.

The bald eagle, while seemingly on its way to population stability, still faces threats. Illegal shooting is the most often recorded cause of eagle deaths. Others die from lead poisoning caused by feeding on carrion riddled with lead shot, or are hit by vehicles while they feed on road-killed animals. Still others collide with high-tension power lines, although many power companies have redesigned wiring patterns to minimize bird mortality.

Conservationists have to be cheered by success stories. Eagles have returned to abandoned breeding grounds. In 1987, a bald eagle nest in Tennessee produced young for the first time since eagles disappeared from the state decades ago. In 1989, there were eleven active nests in Tennessee and the first recorded instance of bald eagles nesting in Kansas was celebrated.

EAGLE ACTIVITIES

- Develop a web with the topic "Bald Eagle." Use such subtopics as national symbol, predator, Native Americans, DDT, economic significance, etc. The web might look like the one in figure 9.4.

Eagles and Native Americans

- The eagle has always been a special symbol for Native American tribes. Research the role of the eagle feather as part of the costumes of Native Americans. Write a short report based on your research, including a drawing of an eagle feather.

- Research the use of the eagle feather in Native American headdresses. Design a headdress based on your research.

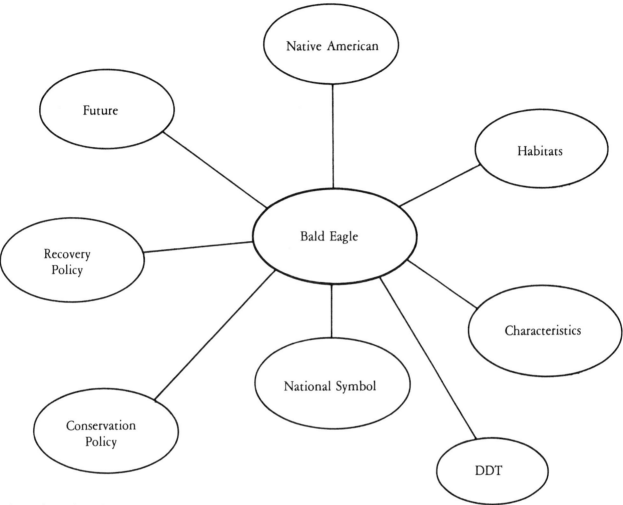

Fig. 9.4. Eagle web.

- Research Native American dances that can be performed in public. If possible, arrange for a Native American to share and teach the class one or more of these dances.

Eagles as Symbols

- The eagle is a symbol of the United States of America. Find out the many ways in which the eagle is used, for example, on the Great Seal, on money, and so forth. Prepare a bulletin board that displays the use of the symbol, as well as appropriate magazine and newspaper articles.

- Research the controversy surrounding the adoption of the eagle as the United States symbol in 1782. Benjamin Franklin supported the wild turkey as the national symbol. Think of other appropriate symbols, prepare arguments for the adoption of each, and discuss in class.

- Design a coin using the turkey or other animals that were suggested as symbols.

- Many other countries have used the eagle as their symbol. For example, ancient Egypt and Russia used the double-headed eagle as a symbol of power. Research these and other civilizations that have honored the eagle. Make a collage or other display of these countries' uses of the symbol.

- Research sports teams that use the eagle as a symbol, such as the Philadelphia Eagles.

- Research the use of eagles in radio and television commercials, magazines, and newspaper ads. Create new ads featuring eagles.

Eagles and the Environment

- Visit a natural history museum that has displays on bald eagles. Study the environment of the bald eagle. Make sketches and then develop a diorama that incorporates what you have learned.

- Visit a zoo that has bald eagles. Observe the behavior of the bald eagle in captivity. Research how it would behave in the wild and make a chart comparing behavior in the two environments.

- Research what eagles eat. What effect does this have on the environment? Compare the feeding habits of eagles in the wild and eagles in confinement. Compare their feeding habits to those of other birds. Graph or chart your results.

- Ranchers often accuse eagles of attacking and killing their sheep and cattle. Research this situation using newspapers and magazines. Discuss the impact of these occurrences.

- The use of DDT in the 1940s, 1950s, and 1960s did much to reduce the population of bald eagles. Research how DDT affected the eagle and what discontinued use of the pesticide did to promote the recovery of the eagle. Research the negative aspects of discontinuing the use of DDT. Compare the advantages to the disadvantages.

- Find out from the Fish and Wildlife Service if there are nesting eagles in your area that you might be able to observe.

- Write to Regional Offices of Endangered Species to get information on the conservation and recovery of the bald eagle. Find out what programs in your area are in action to help the bald eagle population. Addresses of these offices are:

    Regional Office of Endangered Species
    U.S. Fish and Wildlife Service
    Lloyd 500 Building, Suite 1692
    500 N.E. Multnomah Street
    Portland, OR 97232

    Regional Office of Endangered Species
    U.S. Fish and Wildlife Service
    P.O. Box 1306
    Albuquerque, NM 87103

Regional Office of Endangered Species
U.S. Fish and Wildlife Service
Federal Building, Fort Snelling
Twin Cities, MN 55111

Regional Office of Endangered Species
U.S. Fish and Wildlife Service
Richard B. Russell Federal Building
75 Spring Street, S.W.
Atlanta, GA 30303

Regional Office of Endangered Species
U.S. Fish and Wildlife Service
One Gateway Center, Suite 700
Newton Corner, MA 02158

Regional Office of Endangered Species
U.S. Fish and Wildlife Service
P.O. Box 25486
Denver Federal Center
Denver, CO 80225

Eagles and the Arts

• Collect all the songs you can identify that include eagles in the title or lyrics. Share them in class. Create new lyrics or a new song that uses the eagle as its theme.

• Make a papier-mâché model of a bald eagle.

• Make a mural that depicts the bald eagle in its habitat, perhaps with its mate and young.

NOTES

1. *Official World Wildlife Fund Guide to Endangered Species*, volume 2 (*Bald Eagle [Haliaeetus leucocephalus]*) (Washington, D.C.: Beacham Publishing, 1990), 625.

RESOURCE BIBLIOGRAPHY

Books

Baker, Lucy. *Eagles*. New York: Puffin Books, 1990.
    A book for children aged seven to eleven, with facts, games, puzzles, and other activities. Color drawings and photographs illustrate the text.

Brown, Leslie. *Eagles*. New York: Arco Publishing, 1970.
    There are over sixty species of the bird we call *eagle* and they are found on every continent except Antarctica. This book, well-illustrated with photographs and line drawings, details what eagles have in common and some of the differences between species. The author shows the plight of eagles, particularly in industrially developed countries.

General Accounting Office. *Endangered Species: Management Improvements Could Enhance Recovery Program*. GAO/RCED-89-5. Washington, D.C.: General Accounting Office, 1988.

Isaacson, Philip M. *The American Eagle*. Boston: New York Geographic Society, 1975.
This book places the eagle in historical perspective in its transformation as an American symbol. A history of the eagle motif is given in charming detail. The book also serves as a guide to great American artworks featuring eagles, from museums to private collections to buildings.

Official World Wildlife Fund Guide to Endangered Species. volume 2, *Bald Eagle* (*Haliaeetus leucocephalus*), 624-27. Washington, D.C.: Beacham Publishing, 1990.
This reference is a standard for learning about the description, behavior, habitat, current distribution, and conservation and recovery programs concerning endangered species.

Patent, Dorothy Hinshaw. *Where the Bald Eagles Gather*. New York: Clarion Books, 1984.
The author gives a natural history of the bald eagle and reports on the hundreds of eagles that gather every year on McDonald Creek in Glacier National Park, Montana, to feed on spawning salmon. Action black-and-white photographs accompany the text.

Roever, J. M., and Wilfried Roever. *The North American Eagles*. Austin, Tex.: Steck-Vaughn, 1973.
The authors give information on the bald and golden eagles of North America. Included is a history of the eagle as symbol of the United States, physical and temperamental characteristics of the eagles, mating and incubation details, and a brief survey of conservation problems.

Sattler, Helen Roney. *The Book of Eagles*. New York: Lothrop, Lee & Shepard, 1989.
The author catalogs eagles; details their prowess as hunters; discusses courting, nesting, and rearing behaviors; and tells of the difficulties eagles have with humans. A glossary includes the natural history of sixty-four eagle species, along with their geographical distribution. The book is beautifully illustrated by Jean Day Zallinger.

Magazine Articles

Dunstan, T. C. "Our Bald Eagle: Freedom's Symbol Survives." *National Geographic* 153, no. 2 (1978): 186-99.
A biology professor reports on ten years of studying the bald eagle. In addition to a brief natural history, the researcher recounts some hazards that have caused a decline in the eagle population, such as chemical contamination of food supply, poaching, accidental shooting, and electrocution by power lines. The author tells of tracking a radio-tagged eagle to learn its range and habits.

Whooping Cranes

THE CRANE WIFE

Based on a Traditional Japanese Folktale

aro lived in the mountains with his very old mother. Taro was a simple but honest man who made his meager living farming. He went to the village rarely, for he seldom had money to spend. One day Taro's mother sent him to market to get some cloth so that she could make clothes for Taro and herself.

On the way to the village market, Taro saw a beautiful crane struggling to free herself from a trap in which she was ensnared. With pity in his heart for the poor creature, he approached the trap and began to set the crane free. Just then the trapper approached and said, "What do you think you are doing? That is my trap and that is my crane. She will make some very nice bed stuffing for me and my family. Get away from my trap."

"Won't you let her go free?" pleaded Taro. "She is so young and beautiful. Think of the years she will spend bringing happiness and luck to our countrymen."

"This is not your business," yelled the trapper. "Now get away from my trap or you will be sorry."

Taro reached in his pocket and pulled out the money he was going to use to buy cloth. "Here. Take this money. I was going to buy cloth but I'll buy this crane if you will let me."

The trapper looked at the money and agreed. Taro, after he had retrieved the crane from the trap, immediately set her free and he watched joyfully as she flew away. He felt good about what he had done but was embarrassed that he would have no cloth to take home to his mother.

Back at their humble hut, Taro explained to his mother what he had done. His mother was disappointed, of course, that she would not have cloth to sew into clothes, but she was proud of her son for his tender heart. "That's all right, Taro," she said, "perhaps we will have a mild winter and our old threadbare clothes will be sufficient."

The next night, a soft knock on the door awakened a dozing Taro. When he opened the door, he was surprised to see a beautiful young woman, who asked if she could spend the night.

"Oh, our home is too modest for such a lovely lady," Taro said. "You deserve to sleep in a palace."

"Your home will serve well," the charming lady replied.

Taro served her a bowl of rice and after the simple meal she began to talk. "I would like to ask something of you, Taro. I would like to be your wife; that is, if you would have me."

Taro was surprised almost beyond belief. He could not imagine that such a beautiful woman would want to marry him. "We are so very poor, as you can see, and I couldn't offer much to a wife," Taro stated matter-of-factly.

"That doesn't matter, Taro," countered the woman. "I am sure that we can be very happy. Isn't that what really matters?"

Taro looked at his mother and at the lovely creature offering herself for marriage. Taro's mother nodded and Taro said, "Nothing would make me happier." And so they were married as winter began.

Taro's mother had been wrong when she jested about the mild winter they might have. The winter was fierce and long. The food supply began to dwindle. The extra mouth to feed, even though it was a gorgeous mouth, seemed to be too much of a drain on the few resources that Taro had.

One day, after a particularly lean meal, Taro's new wife offered a suggestion. "I can weave," she began. "I have watched women in my village work at their looms and I have done some weaving myself. Do you have a loom?"

"Yes," Taro's mother answered, "but I am afraid it is in very bad repair. I have not used it in a long while for I am not a very good weaver."

"It will do nicely," said the wife cheerfully. "I must be left alone, Taro. I will weave in the closet. You must not disturb me, no matter what happens. I will finish a fine bolt of cloth in three days. You can take it to the village and get a high price, for I do extraordinary work."

For three days, Taro heard the *teedle-womp*, *teedle-womp*, *teedle-womp* of the decrepit old loom. On the third day, his wife came out carrying the finest bolt of cloth he or his mother had ever seen. The beautiful young wife looked tired and somehow thinner, though, and Taro urged her to sit and eat immediately.

Taro's trip to the village to sell the cloth was very profitable and he returned with a great deal of money—enough, he thought, to last them through this winter and into the next season. However, Taro's taste began to change. He bought fine things in the village market and started living a more extravagant lifestyle than he or his mother had ever known. Soon his extravagance began to strain his resources and quickly he found himself in the same poor condition that he had known for so long. He asked his wife if she could weave another bolt of cloth so that their conditions might improve.

The faithful wife agreed, but warned that this would be the last time she could weave a bolt of fine cloth. "As before," she said, "I must not be disturbed. No matter what happens, you must not open the door to the closet."

Taro agreed and listened to the *teedle-womp*, *teedle-womp*, *teedle-womp* of the loom for four days and nights. On the fifth day, his wife entered the sitting room carrying a bolt of cloth even finer than the first. She looked very thin and exhausted and a happy Taro invited her to eat the soup his mother had just finished making.

The bolt of cloth brought ten times the amount the first bolt had, for the fame of the beautiful weaver had spread throughout the village. Shoppers were in a frenzy to buy the fine cloth and the bidding went to a level Taro could scarcely imagine. One of the wealthy citizens of the village approached Taro and suggested that he would buy another bolt of cloth at a hundred times the price the second bolt had brought.

"I don't know," Taro lamented. "This was to be the last bolt. I'll have to ask my wife."

"Nonsense," goaded the rich villager, "are you the man of your house? Here's all the money in advance. You are now among the wealthiest of the village. You can buy a new house, new clothes, and even hire you and your wife servants to do the chores."

Taro could not resist the offer. Visions of wealth overwhelmed his reason and he took the money from the villager. Before he left the village he bought fine clothes for himself, some wonderful knickknacks for his house, some fine jewelry for himself, his wife, and his mother, and even a donkey to carry all the things home. He made the trip home in joy, eager to show his wife and mother the fine things he had bought for them. Still, his happiness was tinged with the dread of telling his wife that she must weave one more bolt of cloth, for he knew that the weaving took a lot out of his wife.

Taro's wife received the news that she must weave another bolt of cloth with sorrow.

"Because I am a faithful wife, I will do it, Taro, but this will absolutely be the last time. I am not able to do it after this. Do not ask."

"Just this last time," Taro cajoled, pleading with his voice and his eyes.

The wife spoke solemnly. "Do not disturb me at all. No matter what happens, I must not be bothered. This time will take a little longer, but do not, under any circumstance, look in on me."

Taro heard the *teedle-womp*, *teedle-womp*, *teedle-womp* of the loom for a full week. On the eighth day, curiosity got the best of him and he opened the door just a crack so that he could peek at what his wife was doing. He was horrified at what he saw. The room was occupied by a crane who seemed to be in pain as she pulled feathers from her own body to place into the loom.

The crane looked in dismay at the intruder. "Oh, no," she shrieked, "I am undone. I am the crane you saved from the trap last year. I have served as your faithful wife but I can serve no more. I must be away from the human world and return to my bird kingdom. Here is your precious bolt of cloth. Take it to the villager who paid you so handsomely for it. I married you, Taro, for your gentleness and humility, but the money I have made for you has caused you to change. Be happy in the life you have made for yourself. I must go."

With this, the crane, with most of her feathers missing, flew away into the east wind. Taro watched until she was just a speck against the gray sky and then returned to his house, which, though it was filled with treasures, was strangely bitter without the lovely wife he adored.

▶●◀

FOLKLORE

Cranes have a long history in the folklore of most civilizations. Cranes were painted on the walls of Egyptian tombs. Some letters of the Greek alphabet are said to be styled after cranes in flight.

Greek and Roman writers thought cranes to be wise, intelligent, and sociable, able to give help to fallen companions. They believed that cranes in flight propped their bills against one another to rest during the long migration. Also, they thought that large birds carried smaller, weaker birds on their backs during the migration. Classical authors told of a legend in which large cranes battled pygmies who had transformed a maiden into a crane.

The crane is particularly prominent in the folklore, symbolism, and iconography of Asian countries. The likeness of a crane is used in Japanese and Chinese wedding designs as a symbol of longevity and happiness. Chinese art sometimes depicts a crane carrying the soul of a dead person to heaven. Cranes stand for happiness, fidelity, and long life and continue to be revered in Japan and China.

One of the most common art symbols in Japan is a crest featuring an encircled crane's head. One such motif is the logo for Japan Air Lines.

Nine of the fifteen known species of crane are migratory, travelling hundreds or even thousands of miles. By the arrival and departure of migrating cranes, farmers calculated the seasons. Three thousand years ago, Homer spoke of crane migrations in *The Iliad*. To ancient Greek and Roman listeners, the sounds of cranes in the spring was a signal to begin plowing. The crane is mentioned in the Bible as a harbinger of seasons in Jeremiah 8:7: "Yea, the stork in the heaven knoweth her appointed times; and the turtle and the crane and the swallow observe the time of their coming." Because cranes were thought to carry spring into the winter landscape, the red on their heads became a symbol of the sun.

The crane dance is mentioned in Greek literature and practiced in Europe and Asia as a fertility rite associated with the warmth of spring. Traditionally, these dances, consisting of bowing, running, and jumping, emulated the courtship dances of cranes. Through participation, the dancers symbolized a renewal of life with the joys and passions of springtime cranes.

Cranes were also considered weather prophets. Reportedly, they were able to call forth storms with their cries. In fall, the early passage of cranes foretold an early winter. When cranes turned back from a sea crossing, sailors were reluctant to leave port. Theophrastus suggested that when cranes left and did not return, it was a sign of fair weather.

Simple folk have commonly regarded cranes as more intelligent than humans.

A modern-day folktale centers around a Japanese girl, Sadako, who lived in Hiroshima when the atomic bomb was dropped near the end of World War II. She became fatally ill from the high radiation dose she received. She felt that she had a mission in the few remaining months of her life to bring the message of peace to the world. As an instrument, she chose the ancient symbol of the crane and began to fold paper cranes using the Japanese *origami* method. Her goal was to fold a thousand cranes and place them in Hiroshima's monument to peace. Unfortunately, she died before her mission was completed. However, others took up her task, not only in Hiroshima and other cities in Japan, but in the entire world. Now, on August 6, the anniversary of the bombing of Hiroshima, hundreds of thousands of paper cranes sent from around the world are placed on the memorial.

DISCUSSION

Description

The whooping crane (*Grus americana*) is the tallest of North American birds, the adult male standing 4½ feet (126 centimeters) tall and weighing about 16 pounds (7.3 kilograms). Adult "whoopers" are white and have red facial skin on the crown and sides of the head. The tips of the wings are black. The bill is dark gray, but becomes lighter in color as the breeding season nears. Legs and feet are usually black.

Behavior

The whooping crane reaches sexual maturity between four and six years of age, at which time it mates for life. Premating behavior, which consists of dancing displays, begins on their wintering grounds near the end of winter. Pairs begin arriving at the breeding grounds (Wood Buffalo National Park in Canada's Northwest Territories) in late April and they return to the same nesting site year after year.

In late April or early May, the female lays two eggs, olive-buff in color and covered with dark, purplish-brown blotches. Both parents share in the incubation duty, with the female sitting on the nest by night and the male by day. After a chick hatches, in about a month, the parents tend the nest closely for about twenty days.

Whoopers begin their southward migration in mid-September, stopping along the way to feed and rest. By mid-November, they arrive at their wintering grounds on the southern Texas coast (Aransas National Wildlife Refuge), where they spend about six months. They feed on blue crabs found on flooded tidal flats and in sloughs. As the flats drain, the cranes move to shallow bays and channels, where they feed on clams. Later in the season, they move inland to feed on seeds, notably acorns.

Habitat

Nesting sites are in dense, low-lying vegetation in marshes or along lakes. The Wood Buffalo National Park in the Canadian Northwest Territories is a vast, 11-million-acre (44,500 square kilometer) refuge in which the whooping cranes have relative peace and quiet. The birds are intolerant of humans and other disturbing influences, particularly during the nesting season, and need the serenity that this setting gives. The nesting site of the whoopers was unknown for years and was finally located only in 1954. Since then, human activity in the area has been on the rise, with overflights of fixed-wing aircraft, fly-bys of helicopters, and banding of the young becoming a summer ritual. Evidently whooping cranes have necessarily become more tolerant of disturbances. Former nesting sites were more southward, extending into Minnesota, Wisconsin, and Iowa. Wood Buffalo Park is the final retreat.

The crane's wintering grounds are flats, marshes, and barrier islands along the Texas coast at Aransas National Wildlife Refuge. In years past, whoopers wintered in Mexico, all along the Texas coast and into Louisiana, and in Florida. Consolidation in the past few decades has placed the main flock exclusively at Aransas. Salt grass dominates the marsh plants on that wintering ground. Inland portions of the winter habitat include scrubby trees (mainly live oak) and various long-stemmed grasses.

Historic Range and Current Distribution

The whooping crane once ranged over most of North America, from the Arctic Circle to central Mexico and from Utah east to the Atlantic coast. Within historic times, the breeding range extended from Manitoba to the north-central United States. (See fig. 10.1.)

Whoopers used to winter all along the Gulf coast in Texas and northeastern Mexico, as well as on the interior tablelands of western Texas and high plateaus of central Mexico. The principal historic wintering grounds were the tall grass prairies of southwestern Louisiana around White Lake. There the primary flock returned year after year. Several of the flock became nonmigrants, spending both summer and winter at the Louisiana lake. A severe tropical storm in August of 1940 decimated the flock, sending them into a fatal decline. In 1950, the last of the Louisiana cranes—a male named "Mac"—was captured and transported to the Aransas Refuge. Unfortunately, he was not accepted by the Aransas cranes and, although he was looked after and relocated within the refuge, he died within six months.

The Wood Buffalo National Park (Northwest Territories) is the last known nesting area for the Canadian population of whooping cranes. This population numbered 138 birds in 1989. The wintering grounds are the Aransas National Wildlife Refuge on the coast of southern Texas. A small breeding population of fifteen to twenty whooping cranes being raised by sandhill cranes summers at Gray's Lake National Wildlife Refuge in Idaho. This flock winters in New Mexico at the Bosque del Apache National Wildlife Refuge and near Chihuahua, Mexico. Experimental breeding populations are maintained at Patuxent Wildlife Research Center at Laurel, Maryland; at the International Crane Foundation in Baraboo, Wisconsin; and at the San Antonio Zoo in Texas. The total population of whooping cranes, captive and wild, is only about 300.

Reasons for Endangerment and Attempts to Help

The whooping crane is certainly one of the best known of endangered birds and is a symbol of the programs in the United States and Canada to save all endangered species. The tallest bird in North America had been rare for some time, but the problem became widely known in 1941, when the entire crane population numbered only twenty-one individuals.

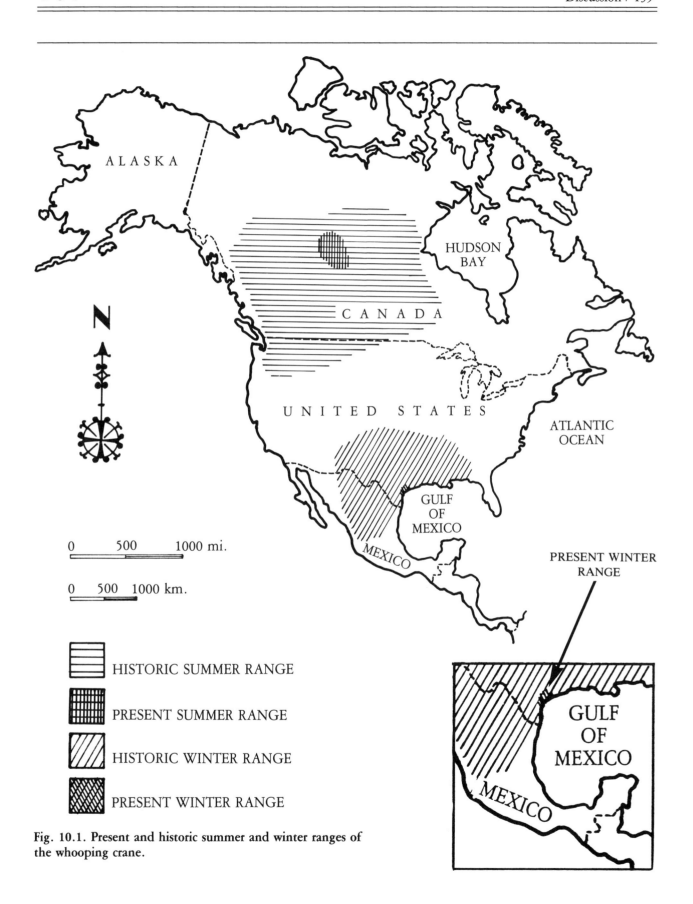

Fig. 10.1. Present and historic summer and winter ranges of
the whooping crane.

Whooping cranes at one time were widely distributed across North America, but the cultivation of the midwestern prairies forced the crane to retreat much farther north for nesting. The establishment of Wood Buffalo National Park in 1922 gave the whooping crane an undisturbed area for nesting. The founding of the park was not, however, an overt attempt to help the crane. It was not discovered that the whoopers used the site as a nesting area until 1954.

On December 31, 1937, President Franklin Delano Roosevelt signed an executive order declaring the 47,000 acres in the Aransas area a national wildlife preserve. This presidential order saved the whooping crane. At that time only two small flocks survived, one a migratory flock of about fourteen birds that wintered on the "Aransas Migratory Waterfowl Refuge," as it was then called. A second flock of about twelve wintered at isolated but unprotected marshes around White Lake, Louisiana. As noted, a storm in 1940 halved that population.

Part of the problem is the cranes' reproductive capacity. A female usually lays two fertile eggs, but almost always only one chick survives. Evidently a pair of crane parents can find food to support only one chick, so the weaker of the pair dies. Also, the cranes have always migrated over a 3,000-mile-long route from northern Canada to southern Texas. That path carries the birds through Canada and the states of North and South Dakota, Nebraska, Kansas, Oklahoma, and Texas, over cities, highways, and industrial complexes. Hazards along the way include hunters, high-tension electrical wires, and poisoning from pesticide-laden grain. All these dangers, combined with the marginal nesting skills of whooping cranes, made them susceptible to rapid population declines and near-extinction as a species.

Propagation of a captive flock of whooping cranes has been ongoing since 1966, when the Patuxent Wildlife Research Center was formed at Laurel, Maryland. This flock numbers about thirty. Eggs taken from this captive flock, as well as some from Canada, were introduced to sandhill crane nests in 1975. The idea—a tactic that seems to have worked at least in part—was to press the sandhill cranes into service for the incubation and rearing of whooper chicks. The sandhills would act as foster parents until the whoopers reached sexual maturity. It was hoped that the whoopers would then mate with their own kind and reproduce. The sandhills have in fact accepted the whooping crane chicks as their own and have taught the larger birds the sandhill's migratory flyway, a much shorter and safer route from Gray's Lake National Wildlife Refuge in southern Idaho to the Bosque del Apache National Wildlife Refuge in southern New Mexico. This project started with fourteen eggs. Nine of the whooping cranes hatched that first season, but four were killed in various ways. In 1976, five whooping cranes were spotted among the sandhill flock at the wintering home in the south. However, the whooping cranes that survived mated and never produced young, so the project was abandoned.

The Fish and Wildlife Service intends to introduce populations of whooping cranes in several sites in the eastern United States. Prime candidates are the Okefenokee swamp of southern Georgia and the Kissimmee prairie of Florida. The Canadian Wildlife Service published a Whooping Crane Recovery Plan in 1988 and plans to start its own breeding population. More information on these programs may be obtained from:

Regional Office of Endangered Species
U.S. Fish and Wildlife Service
P.O. Box 1306
Albuquerque, NM 87103

CRANE ACTIVITIES

Cranes and the Environment

- Using a map of North America, show the winter and summer ranges of the whooping crane and its traditional migratory routes.

- Research the migratory habits of the whooping crane from the Northwest Territories to the Texas coast. Then create a journal that details the dates, sights, weather, geology, and so forth along the route.

- Sandhill cranes were used as surrogate parents for some whooping crane eggs. The presence of a handfull of white whooping cranes among some 20,000 darker-colored sandhill cranes that migrate annually can be seen in March in the San Luis Valley near Monte Vista, Colorado. They rest in the marshes as they return from their winter home in the Bosque del Apache National Wildlife Refuge in New Mexico to summer nesting grounds in Idaho, Montana, and Wyoming. Plan a trip to see the greater and lesser sandhill cranes and their few adopted whooping cranes either in New Mexico or Colorado. Use a map to determine the route(s) you take. Estimate the mileage. What other attraction(s) might you want to see along the way? Ask a librarian or travel agent to help you get information. Make a budget for expected expenses.

- Create a dialogue between two whooping cranes, comparing their journeys from the Wood Buffalo National Park in Canada's Northwest Territories to the Aransas National Wildlife Refuge on the Gulf Coast of Texas.

- Make a diorama that depicts the whooping crane in its Wood Buffalo or Aransas Refuge habitat.

Cranes as an Endangered Species

- Detail some of the factors that have brought the whooping crane to near-extinction and some of the efforts that have caused the population to increase. Make a report or publish a newsletter on your findings.

- A significant amount of public money is spent on protecting the whooping crane population. Decide if the expenditure is worth it. Organize a class discussion that presents both sides.

Cranes as Symbols

- The crane is the basis for the logo of Japan Air Lines. Research why the crane is a significant symbol for this business.

- Think of a business that could logically use the crane as a symbol. Design a crane logo for the business.

Cranes and the Arts

- The illustration of the whooping crane that accompanies this chapter shows the cranes in their graceful mating dance. Learn more about this dance. Use the information to choreograph a dance for humans that uses the movements of the whooping crane.

- Sandhill cranes are used as surrogate parents for some whooping cranes. Fertilized eggs of the whoopers are set under nesting sandhills. The hatched whoopers are "adopted" by the sandhills and raised as their own, even though the whooper young are considerably different from sandhills. Write an episode for a situation comedy television show in which sandhill crane parents must cope with the struggles of raising "difficult" offspring.

- Write a poem about whooping cranes. Use the haiku form, which consists of three lines: the first line has five syllables, the second line has seven syllables, and the third line has five syllables.

- Write and perform a rap song about whooping cranes. Include in your rap song the plight of the crane and the conservation efforts.

- Write a choral reading piece about the whooping crane. You could have some individuals perform verses of the reading and provide a chorus with the sounds of the flying cranes; for example:

Reader 1:	High in the sky
Chorus:	Whooooo, Whooooo
Reader 2:	The whooping cranes fly.
Chorus:	Whooooo, Whooooo
Reader 3:	Could they be so happy
Chorus:	Whooooo, Whooooo
Reader 4:	As you and I?
Chorus:	Whooooo, Whooooo
	Whooooo, Whooooo, Whooooo, Whooooo!

- Draw a mural of several whooping cranes in their habitat in the Aransas National Wildlife Refuge.

- Search your newspaper for stories dealing with whooping cranes. Use these articles to make a bulletin-board display.

- Publish a newspaper edition about the whooping crane. Include stories, natural history, cartoons, jokes, riddles, illustrations, and poems.

- Make a full-scale papier-mâché model of a whooping crane.

RESOURCE BIBLIOGRAPHY

Books

Bang, Molly. *The Paper Crane*. New York: Greenwillow, 1985.
   The author uses photographs of three-dimensional artwork to illustrate this classic folktale.
   A struggling restaurateur offers food to an apparently poor and hungry stranger, who leaves
   a paper napkin folded into the shape of a crane as a gift, with the promise that a clap of the
   hands will bring the bird to life. The living magical crane serves as an attraction that restores
   the restaurant's failing business. Patrons continue to come even after the mysterious
   stranger returns, plays a tune on a flute while the crane dances, then climbs on the crane's
   back as they both fly away.

Coerr, Eleanor. *Sadako and the Thousand Paper Cranes*. New York: G. P. Putnam's Sons, 1977.
   This book tells the compelling and poignant true story of Sadako, a twelve-year-old victim
   of the atomic bomb blast at Hiroshima near the close of World War II. The stricken girl
   makes paper cranes as therapy, believing that the making of a thousand cranes will aid her
   healing. Sadly, she did not live to make all the cranes, but her courage has made her a
   heroine in Japan, especially to the children. Paintings by Ronald Himler illustrate the book.

Doughty, Robin W. *Return of the Whooping Crane*. Austin, Tex.: University of Texas Press,
   1989.
   This book gives probably the most complete information about whooping cranes available
   in an easy-to-read format. All aspects of the bird are discussed: the crane in folklore, the
   near-vanishing of the species, the slow road to recovery, and the exciting prospects for a
   future of which whooping cranes are a part. A comprehensive bibliography is available for
   the avid reader or researcher who wants to find virtually all the information printed about
   this highly recognizable bird.

McNulty, Faith. *Peeping in the Shell: A Whooping Crane Is Hatched*. New York: Harper &
   Row, 1986.
   The author recounts every detail of the hatching of a whooping crane egg at the Crane
   Research Center at Baraboo, Wisconsin. She describes the "courtship" or dancing that an
   ornithologist, George Archibald, performed with the captive female, Tex, and Tex's artificial insemination with frozen sperm from the Patuxent Wildlife Research Center in Maryland. The fertilized egg that resulted was carefully incubated and finally produced a new
   whooper.

Patent, Dorothy Hinshaw. *The Whooping Crane: A Comeback Story*. New York: Clarion
   Books, 1988.
   This highly regarded author tells the story of the whooping crane, including all the "tricks"
   that are used to allow whoopers to be incubated by sandhill cranes, raised by humans as
   well as sandhills, and still be imprinted as whooping cranes. The perils of having such a
   small population of whooping cranes are discussed, as are nesting, feeding, and migrating.

Seki, Keigo, ed. *Folktales of Japan*. Translated by Robert J. Adams. Chicago, Ill.: University of
   Chicago Press, 1963.
   This volume features a variety of Japanese folktales that have been handed down from
   generation to generation, including those featuring cranes. The most popular of these tales
   have been told in hundreds of different versions, many going back centuries. Seki, a well-
   known folktale scholar, compiled the standard classification of Japanese tales, *Nihon
   Mukashi-banashi Shusei*, based on collections made during this century.

Yagawa, Sumiko. *The Crane Wife*. Translated from the Japanese by Katherine Paterson. Illustrated by Suekichi Akara. New York: William Morrow, 1981.
This beautiful version of the crane wife tale was the winner of the Hans Christian Andersen Medal for illustration. The story of the crane wife is among the most popular in Japanese folktales dealing with nonhuman or enchanted brides. In this version, a simple farmer rescues a wounded crane from death. The crane assumes human form to marry this good man. The farmer is content with his life and his wife, but aspires to more when he discovers that the cloth she weaves brings a princely sum at the market. His greed escalates and he finally loses his lovely wife to her crane world.

Newspaper Articles

Gray, Mary Taylor. "Whoopers Dot Colorado Flock." *The Denver Post* (March 3, 1991): 10T.

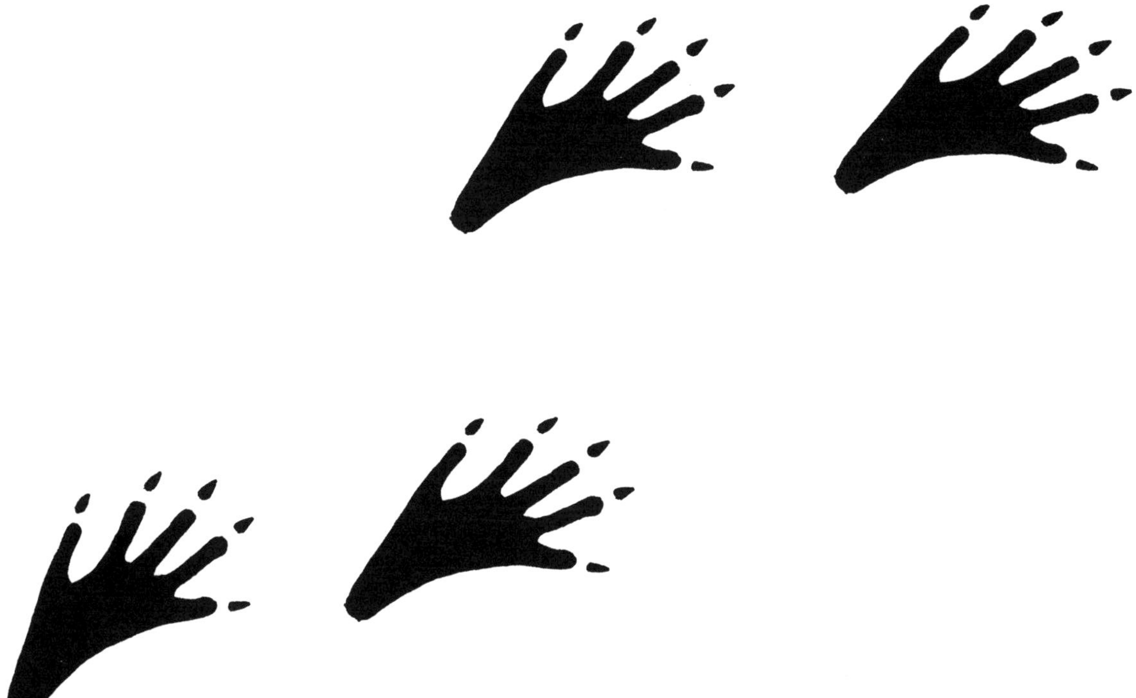

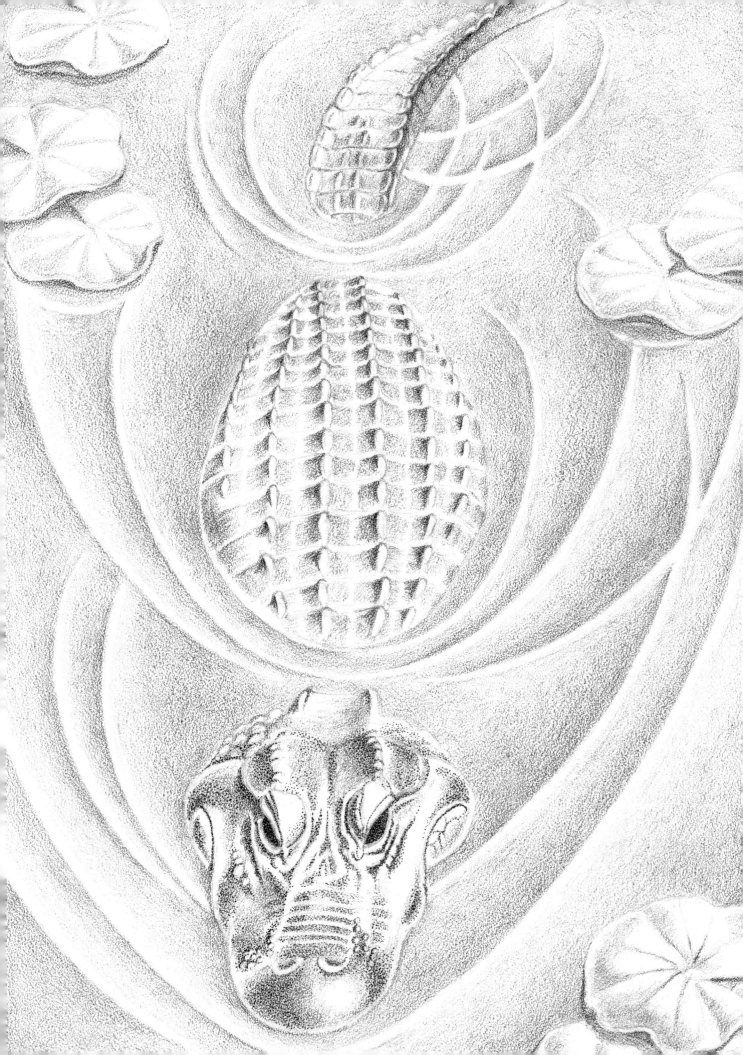

Alligators

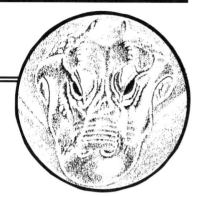

WHY THE ALLIGATOR'S HIDE IS BLACK AND CRINKLY AS A BURNT LOG

South Carolina Folkstory

 long time ago, down by the hot mudbank of the river at the edge of the rice field, there lived an alligator. In those days the proud alligator had a hide that was smooth and white, like catfish skin. Back then the alligator ate the creatures that lived in the water and never bothered animals that lived on the land. Of course, if some careless animal should fall into the river, then it became food for the alligator.

Alligator was out sunning himself on the riverbank when Brer Rabbit stopped to pass the time of day in conversation with him. Old Alligator thought Brer Rabbit was a ridiculous creature, but that didn't stop Alligator from talking with him.

"How are your wife and all the young alligators doing?" asked Brer Rabbit.

Old Alligator didn't really care to know about Brer Rabbit and his kin and wasn't really too interested in talking with him, but he answered, "They're getting along fine. They are bright, smart, and pretty. That's because we raised them the right way right here in the river. They're not like all of you other foolish critters that don't live in the water. You-all spend your time skirmishing round the river and must be worn out before the day is half over."

This superior attitude offended Brer Rabbit. He decided to pretend that Alligator was talking truth instead of just being set in his ways. So Rabbit just sighed, shook his head, and replied sadly, "You might be right. We-all are surely seeing lots of trouble lately."

"What kind of trouble?" asked Alligator.

Brer Rabbit, acting as if he couldn't believe his ears, cried out, "Come on now, Old Alligator. Haven't you heard of Trouble?"

147

"Honestly, Rabbit. I don't know about this Trouble. What does Trouble look like?" asked Alligator.

"Ah, come on, Alligator. As old as you are, you must have seen Trouble!" insisted Rabbit.

"I tell you, Brer Rabbit, I don't know anything about this here Trouble. What does Trouble look like? How does he stand?" puzzled Alligator.

Brer Rabbit just scratched his head. He figured if Alligator was so stupid and self-satisfied about himself and was always so rude about those who lived on the land, maybe this was a chance to put Alligator in his place. Mischievous Brer Rabbit started to scheme about how he was going to have some real fun with Old Alligator. "I don't know that I can tell you exactly how Trouble stands but maybe you would like to see him yourself."

Alligator got interested. "Sure enough. I'd like to see Trouble very much."

"Of course I can show you Trouble, Alligator, but maybe you won't like him so much. I don't know if I should show him to you."

"Hey, Brer Rabbit, I'm not scared of any of that. If I don't like him it won't matter to me at all."

Then Brer Rabbit started to pretend and make excuses. "Well, Old Alligator, I'm pretty busy right now."

"Look here, Rabbit. You have lots of time for messing around and after all, this is me, Old Alligator, asking you. Don't forget who I am!"

Brer Rabbit mocked Old Alligator. "Sure. Of course. How could I ever forget that?" Old Alligator never saw that Brer Rabbit meant mischief. "But I have to fix my house and my wife is feeling poorly, and the children need to be tended to and—"

"Shucks! All that stuff will take care of itself." Old Alligator began to beg and try to persuade Brer Rabbit. He pleaded and begged until at last Brer Rabbit agreed to show him Trouble.

"Well, since you insist. Meet me in this same place as soon as the dew dries off the grass next Saturday. That will be a good day. Maybe Trouble will have some time off Saturday." With that, Brer Rabbit bade Old Alligator good morning and started to leave.

When Saturday came, Old Alligator got up before daybreak, early in the morning, and started to get all fixed up. His wife woke up and asked, "Where are you going?"

Old Alligator didn't crack his teeth at her but kept fixing himself up. That just made his wife even more curious. "Where are you going?" she asked again. She questioned him and questioned him for a long time until Old Alligator knew she was determined to know.

At last he answered, "I'm going with Brer Rabbit."

"Where are you two going?" she asked.

Old Alligator just admired his face in the water and paid her no attention. His wife knew how to get around him and she kept pestering him until he told her, "I am going to see Trouble."

"What is Trouble?" she wanted to know.

"How do I know? That's what I'm going to find out."

She wheedled, "Can I go along too?"

Old Alligator told her no, but she talked, pleaded, and worked on persuading him until finally he lost his patience and said, "All right. You can come along."

So Mrs. Alligator started to get ready to go. While she was doing that she kept talking, until finally the little alligators woke up. They looked at Old Alligator and their mother getting ready to go out. "Where are you going, Daddy?" they asked.

Old Alligator was really exasperated by this time. "It is none of your business," he snapped.

So the little alligators went over to their mother and cried out one after another, "Where are you going, Mother?"

All she would tell them was, "Go away and leave me alone!"

"Daddy, Mother said you were going to tell us where you are going," they teased.

Old Alligator was put out, but he could see it was no use to keep quiet, so he told them, "I'm going to see Trouble."

"Daddy, Daddy, Daddy, can we go? Please let us go! We want to go too," hollered the children, as they all jumped up and down.

Old Alligator roared, "No!"

With that, all the little alligators went to their mother and asked, begged, and pleaded, "Mother, can we go? Can we go? Can we go?"

Finally Mrs. Alligator told them, "If your daddy says you can go, then you can go."

They hurried back to Old Alligator and whined, "Mother said we can go if you let us. Please let us go."

Old Alligator was worn out by this time. "Well then, yes! You can go. But you have to get fixed up nice and remember your manners. You have to show Brer Rabbit how much better behaved water children are than children who live in the woods."

They scurried around getting fixed up and all dressed up. They put on their best, added mud to their heads, marsh on their backs, and moonshine on their tails. "We look really fine now," they all said.

Just about this time Old Alligator looked out and saw that the dew was almost off the grass, so he called to his wife and children, "Come on!"

They all crowded on the bank of the river by the rice field to wait for Brer Rabbit. They weren't there too long before they saw Brer Rabbit coming along, smoking his pipe. When Brer Rabbit got there, he was surprised to see the whole family. He laughed to himself but didn't say anything except, "Howdy." Then he added, "My, how nice the children are all looking." But all the time he saying to himself, "Lordy, this is an ugly gang of people. Look how poor their clothes are! That alligator wife is a real hussy."

Old Alligator never even apologized to Brer Rabbit for bringing along such a crowd. "They all begged me so hard I had to give in and let them come along."

"There is plenty of room for all. I hope you all enjoy yourselves," was Brer Rabbit's answer.

"Thank you, thank you, thank you," they all told Brer Rabbit. The children were all so pleased that Brer Rabbit hadn't sent them home that they danced around in wild joy.

Brer Rabbit thought they all looked so comical, raising their noses and their tails, that it was all he could do to keep from laughing in their faces. He squinted up his face and looked very solemnly at his watch. "I reckon it is time to go along," was all he said to them.

They all started down the rice field bank with Brer Rabbit leading, followed by Old Alligator. Mrs. Alligator came behind all the little ones to make sure they behaved themselves. Did those little ones mind their mother? No way. They dawdled, played, fought, and refused to listen to her. She was quite distracted by them.

Brer Rabbit led them through a patch of woods to an old field that was all grown up full of broom grass and briar. The grass was so thick you could hardly see around in it. It was all dry as tinder and yellow as pure gold. The path they were on took them right spang through this big golden field. When they got to the middle of the field, Brer Rabbit stopped. He took the pipe out of his mouth, put his hand to his ear, and pretended to listen. It looked as if he were hearing something. "Sh! Sh!" he told the young ones.

Mrs. Alligator caught up to them and said, "Sh! Sh! Or I'll lick the tar out of you all."

Brer Rabbit just listened some more and then he shouted, "Who is that calling Brer Rabbit?" He made out like he heard something more and then he yelled back, "Yes. It is me. What do you want with me?" He put his hand to his ear again and then said, "I'm coming right now." With that he turned to Old Alligator. "Somebody is calling me away on business for a minute. Please excuse me and wait right where you are until I can get back to you."

"We'll all stay right here," Old Alligator promised.

Brer Rabbit made a low bow and ran along the path out of sight. That deceitful rascal went till he got to the edge of the woods and set himself down and sniggered to himself like he was tasting the fun before he even started it. Then he got down to business. He smelled the wind to see what direction it was coming from. He pulled up a handful of that long, dry broom grass and knocked a hot coal from his pipe so that the grass caught fire. He ran along the edge of the field with his torch and set fire to the field the whole way around. When he had finished, he got up on a safe, high stump where he had a good view and sat down to wait.

All this time the alligator family was down in the middle of the field. They weren't used to all this travel on the ground and they were tired. "Let's rest awhile. We walked a long piece," suggested Old Alligator. His wife started her pestering again.

"Which way are we going to find Trouble? Why didn't you make Brer Rabbit tell you more about this thing you are looking for? How long do we have to wait?"

Old Alligator didn't give her any answers. He just sat still and grunted every now and again. Once in a while Mrs. Alligator called to the children, "Stop all of that ruckus." And so they sat and they sat and they sat.

The fire burned and raced until at last the wind caught it and it flared up high. A spark and flame flew up, way up into the sky. One of the little alligators saw it and hollered, "Look there! Look there! Look there!" Just as he was going to ask his mother and daddy another question, his mother hushed him up sharply.

The other little alligators looked where their brother alligator had pointed and started to sing out too, "Look there! Look there! Look there!" One of them got an idea and hollered, "Must be Trouble."

Mrs. Alligator finally looked too and then she turned to Old Alligator and quizzed him, "Look, Pa. Is that Trouble for sure?"

Now Old Alligator lived in water and mud and he had never seen fire until now, so he was ignorant and didn't know. However, he didn't feel easy in his mind about what he saw. "Reckon maybe Brer Rabbit got lost or something?"

One of the children shouted, "Trouble is pretty! Trouble is pretty! Trouble is pretty!" With that all of the youngsters sang out, "Trouble is pretty! Trouble is pretty! Trouble is pretty!"

Old Alligator said, "If that is Trouble, he is surely pretty! You children speak the truth." He and his wife ogled the big flames up in the air, watching the fire come closer, and they forgot all about Brer Rabbit. They all stared at the fire and kept quiet for a change because they were afraid they might scare Trouble away. At last a hot spark landed right on the back of one of the little alligators. He squalled and cried, "Trouble hurts! Trouble hurts! Trouble hurts!"

His mother smacked him on his jaw and told him, "Mind your manners and be quiet. Look how pretty Trouble is." Just as she said this, a heavy spark landed on her and burned her badly. She started to jump and holler and bounce around. "It is true. Trouble hurts! Trouble hurts for sure! Oh! Oh! Oh!"

They all remembered Brer Rabbit. "Brer Rabbit, we don't want to see any more Trouble. Brer Rabbit, oh, Brer Rabbit!" they yelled.

By this time the sparks were flying everywhere and the alligators didn't know what to do or where to go. They all ran around and around this way and that way, trying to get out. Everywhere they turned there was fire. They hollered out to Brer Rabbit, "Brer Rabbit! Where are you? Call to Trouble, Brer Rabbit. Come for us! Oh, oh, oh, Brer Rabbit!"

Brer Rabbit didn't come to them and he didn't say anything. The fire got so close to that alligator family that they couldn't holler or stay there anymore. They quit calling for Brer Rabbit and got ready to break through the fire as best they could. They had no other thought in their heads but to get home. Mother Alligator shouted, "Children, follow your daddy!"

With Mother Alligator herding them, they burst right through the scorching fire. They ran through the hot fire, while it blistered and frizzled them, until they finally got through. They had raced past Brer Rabbit just scuttling along. He thought they looked so comical he almost fell off his stump from laughing so hard.

"Old Alligator! I guess you saw Trouble now! Get back in the water where you belong. Don't never, never, hunt Trouble," he chortled.

The alligators were too busy running to stop and argue with him. In fact, they didn't stop until they got to the bank of the river by the rice field and all jumped into the water. They were still so hot from the fire that, when the water hit them, they heard "Swiish-ssssssh-sh!" Pure steam rose up from them in a cloud. They didn't come out again all that day or all that night. The next day, when they had a chance to look at one another, they found that their white skins were just as black and crinkly as burned logs of wood and rough as the bark of a live-oak tree. The alligator family really got tricked that day and from that day to this one, alligators have had horny hides.

►●◄

FOLKLORE

The alligator is the object of dread, reverence, propitiatory gestures, and worship in most regions where it is found. Some Panamanian natives worship an alligator god that has a human body and legs but an alligator head. Sobek, the crocodile god of ancient Egypt, gradually evolved from a minor protective god into one of the most important of all the Egyptian deities.

One voodoo song tells that the queen of voodoo, Marie Laveau, went to school with the alligators. Southern beliefs held that one could avoid witches by wearing a necklace of alligator teeth. A visiting nocturnal witch would have to stop and count every one of the teeth before she could get on with her witchy business, and day would come to banish her before she could count all the teeth. Alligator teeth strung on thread were also believed to be a charm against pain in teething babies. Teeth are also important inclusions in a New Guinea sorcerer's bag. Gullah beliefs teach that when the alligator roars for rain, rain comes. (Alligators roar only in the spring.) The Choctaw Indians venerate the alligator and never kill it. They have a night dance with three songs dedicated to the alligator. Indians in Paraguay tell of an alligator ferryman who carries souls to the afterworld.

One Louisiana story says that the alligator could once whistle, talk, and bark. He loaned his tongue to the dog, but the dog never returned the tongue to the alligator, and that is why an alligator will attack any dog that comes to the bank of the river.

In August 1991, the cartoonist, Mike Peters, did a series of cartoons in his "Mother Goose and Grimm" strip related to the urban folktale of alligators in the sewer system. The dog, Grimm, who is a habitual drinker from the toilet bowl, has daily encounters with the toilet alligator. True to the urban folktale, the series includes the information that alligators got into the sewers when pet baby alligators were flushed down the toilet. Brunvand, in his book *The Vanishing Hitchhiker*,[1] gives some of the variations on this folktale and discusses its origin. There may be some truth to this particular story.[2]

DISCUSSION

Description

Alligators belong to the *crocodilia* order, which is divided into three groups: crocodiles, gavials, and alligators. The alligator genus includes the caimans. The alligator (*Alligator mississipiensis*) is a large wetland reptile of significant commercial and scientific value. Alligators have been described as wooded, swimming islands because seeds from trees fall into the small crevices between their scales, germinate there during the alligators' winter hibernation in the mud, and sprout in the spring.

Alligators are massive creatures that can grow up to 19 feet (5.8 meters) in length. They resemble lizards in shape. Their snouts are shorter and blunter than that of the crocodile. Further, the alligator's lower molars clamp into pits in its upper molars. Their eyes are placed high and seem to stick up above their skulls, so they can see above the water while their bodies are submerged. They can walk on their short, strong legs, but they do not use their legs for swimming. For swimming, they move their powerful tails from side to side. Their tough skin is a mottled dull gray and dark olive color. A 12-foot (3.7-meter) male alligator weighs between 450 and 550 pounds (204.3 to 249.7 kilograms).

Behavior

The female alligator builds a nest mound of plant matter and soil that is about 3 feet (1 meter) high and 7 feet (2 meters) across. She digs a hole in the center of the pile, where the nest is wet, and there lays up to fifty eggs. These eggs are white, hard-shelled, and slightly larger than hens' eggs. The young alligators grunt loudly when they are ready to leave the nest. The mother tears open the nest and sometimes helps her young hatch by lifting the eggs into her mouth, where she gently cracks them open by rolling them against the roof of her mouth with her tongue. When first hatched, the young alligators are about 9 inches (23 centimeters) long. Many of these young remain with their mother until the following spring.

During the first six years of their lives, alligators grow about 1 foot (30 centimeters) in length each year. In winter, alligators bury themselves in mud, go into deep holes, or remain resting underwater. They eat many kinds of small animals that live in or near the water, including fish, snakes, frogs, turtles, and small mammals. Large alligators have been known to attack dogs, pigs, and even cattle. They kill their prey by dragging it underwater to drown it and then tearing it to pieces.

Even though an alligator's jaws are very large and strong in closing, once they are shut a person can easily hold them closed with bare hands. Alligators do not normally attack human beings.

Habitat

Alligators live in tropical wetland areas. In southern North America, they thrive in lakes, swamps, rivers, and the Gulf of Mexico.

Historic Range

Alligators live in the waters and lowlands of the southeastern United States. Another species, the Chinese alligator, lives in the lower Yangtze River Valley in China. These Chinese alligators are much like the American alligator in habits and appearance.

Alligators were once common in lakes, swamps, and rivers along the Gulf of Mexico and on the Atlantic coast as far north as North Carolina. They were also found far up the Mississippi River. They ranged in all or parts of Alabama, Arkansas, Florida, Georgia, Louisiana, Mississippi, Oklahoma, North Carolina, South Carolina, and Texas, but today they are seldom found north of Florida. It is estimated that there are 6.7 million acres (27,000 square kilometers) of habitat for alligators in Florida (see fig. 11.1).

Reasons for Endangerment and Attempts to Help

Overhunting, not habitat loss, was the main factor in the decline of the alligator. They were hunted for their hides and also, to some degree, for their meat. Their skins were made into purses, shoes, boots, belts, and other fashion items.

The alligator is one of the conservation movement's success stories. In 1967 the alligator was classified as an endangered species. However, in 1987, this classification was changed to "Threatened Due to Similarity of Appearance." This classification is a means of protecting still-jeopardized crocodilian species that have similar hides. Alligators began to make their comeback as early as 1975 and this new classification recognizes the recovery of the species rangewide.

Regulated harvests of wild alligators are now permitted. Alligator farms, where the reptiles are raised for commercial sale of the hides and meat, have also been developed.

Fig. 11.1. Alligator range (Southeastern United States).

ALLIGATOR ACTIVITIES

Alligators and the Environment

- Research other reptiles, such as crocodiles or caimans. Where do they live and how are they alike and different?

- Research the habitat of alligators. If possible, visit a zoo and sketch any crocodilians residing there. Then create a mural depicting them in their habitat.

- Research how fast alligators move in water compared to their movement on land. Discuss the significance of this difference for others in the same environment.

- In the summer of 1981, a young alligator escaped from the Denver Zoo and found refuge and food in City Park's Duck Lake. He was named Albert the Alligator after the intelligent character in the "Pogo" comic strip. Albert remained free for twenty-eight days, during which time he became notorious. Read the articles about Albert (see fig. 11.2, pages 157-60). Brainstorm activities you could do, such as celebrating Albert's escape with activities specific to alligators, escapes, survival, finding clothing with alligator symbols, and so forth. Research the differences in the two environments and write a story telling why Albert found City Park preferable to the zoo and what humans did to return him to the zoo.

Alligators as an Endangered Species

- Make a chart of the uses of alligator and alligator hides.

- Recent estimates of the price of alligator hide run about $75 per square foot. How much hide would it take to make a belt, purse, shoes, or boots? Estimate the price of one whole hide from an average-sized adult alligator.

Alligators and Literature

- The story of how the alligator got his hide is a *pourquoi* or how/why story. Every culture has stories explaining how things happened. How else might early people have explained the alligator's horny, dark, crinkly, rough hide? Create a new story and illustrate it or illustrate the story in this book. Create a readers' theatre script from your story.

- This American black folkstory is a literal retelling of a Rhodesian story, except that the African version mixes humans into the plot. An Alabama Native American story is similar to the black story. Find Rhodesia and Alabama on a globe. How would you explain the same story being found in both places?

- Read versions of the urban legend about alligators appearing in the sewers of our cities. (Jan Harold Brunvand gives several in his book *The Vanishing Hitchhiker*.) Develop a series of comic strips about this story. (Also refer to the "Mother Goose and Grimm" strips that appeared in August 1991. Check microfilm of daily newspapers in your library.)

(Text continues on page 161.)

Fig. 11.2. "Albert the Alligator" stories. Reprinted with permission of the *Rocky Mountain News*.

Day 16: Elusive reptile remains in hiding

Albert the alligator was still at large Friday, his 16th day of freedom after escaping from the Denver Zoo's alligator pen.

Zoo spokesmen said Albert was still thought to be in City Park's Duck Lake, but the shifty reptile continues to evade his captors. There were no sightings of Albert reported Friday.

July 4, 1981

Albert the alligator keeps low profile

Twenty days have passed as Albert the alligator remained at large Tuesday in City Park's Duck Lake.

The 4-foot reptile, who broke from his quarters in the Denver Zoo nearly three weeks ago, was spotted several times Monday, cruising the lake a dozen feet from shore.

On Tuesday, perhaps because of the excitement he had generated, Albert was keeping a low profile.

"The last we saw him was 6 p.m. Monday, when he was heading back to the zoo side of the lake," said Clayton Freiheit, the zoo's director.

Albert, who has managed to outsmart the best of the zoo's hunters, goes in and out of the zoo at will, apparently under a fence separating the two lakes.

July 8, 1981

Crafty gator adding duck to his menu?

On his 21st day of liberty since escaping from the Denver Zoo, Albert the alligator remained at large Wednesday. One man said he saw Albert eat a duck.

Albert, who has attracted crowds hoping for a glimpse of him, was spotted in the middle of Duck Lake in City Park.

Paul Linger, assistant director of the zoo, said plans are afoot to snare Albert. He would not divulge details.

The alligator is believed to be living mainly on carp, but one witness told radio station KIMN that Wednesday he saw a member of a family of ducks disappear into the gator's capacious jaws.

July 9, 1981

(Fig. 11.2 continues on page 158.)

Fig. 11.2. — *Continued*

Slippery alligator remains on the loose

On his 22nd day of freedom, Albert the alligator cruised through the waters of City Park's Duck Lake, shunning the nearby waters of the Denver Zoo.

Albert has made several escapes from the Zoo since he arrived in early June. Zoo officials believe the 4-foot alligator swims under or climbs over a fence separating the zoo from Duck Lake, but he's never been caught in the act.

Clayton Freiheit, Zoo director, said he saw Albert at 8:30 a.m. Thursday.

Albert nearly was captured on Wednesday. Zoo employee Greg Abbott spotted Albert in one of his favorite hiding spots and headed for him with a catchpole.

Abbott "got the noose over his nose, but Albert managed to shake it loose," Freiheit said.

July 10, 1981

Albert eludes captors once again

By FRANCES MELROSE
News Staff

Albert the alligator chalked up another day of freedom — his 23rd — Friday, foiling a well-mounted attempt to capture him.

The 4-foot alligator gained his freedom by clambering over or swimming under the fence separating the Denver Zoo lake from City Park's Duck Lake more than three weeks ago.

Albert was spotted Friday morning taking a swim about 12 feet offshore in Duck Lake, to the delight of a crowd of 200. Children called, "Hello, Albert." The reptile paddled around smartly, giving them his other profile.

A zoo crew, including assistant director Paul Linger, foreman Rex Williams and keepers Greg Abbott, Archie Paulson, Mike Cervoski and Charles Radcliffe, descended on Albert about 10 a.m. with a seine-type nylon net 25-by-4 feet, weighted with chains and with plastic bottles for floats.

The net was lowered in the area where Albert last lurked. The crew almost had him.

"But he crawled out through the mud underneath," said Williams.

Cervoski, in a small rubber raft, also moved out toward Albert, hoping to drop a catchpole noose over his nose. But the gator spotted that maneuver a long way off and submerged.

"It's all over now," said Williams. "He's spooked. We'll have to come back again after dark, with big searchlights. The hardest thing is getting close to him. We'll flash big lights around until we spot him — his eyes glow like red balls in the light — and then we'll try to get him. We'll give it three tries, but if we miss on all of them, we'll quit and come back another night."

July 11, 1981

Fig. 11.2. — *Continued*

Elusive Albert free another day

Albert, the elusive alligator, chalked up one more day of freedom — his 26th — Monday while Denver Zoo attendants plotted another strategy to capture him.

The 4-foot 'gator has been gliding under a fence separating the zoo pond from City Park's Duck Lake. The chain-link fence had been torn loose at the bottom by scuba divers, according to zoo officials.

Albert was spotted inside the zoo early Monday, but by afternoon he was paddling around Duck Lake entertaining fans who were lining the shores hoping to catch a glimpse of the alligator.

"We had our hands on him Sunday," said zoo director Clayton Freiheit. "Mike Kinsey,

assistant foreman at the zoo, got him surrounded with a net, and one of the keepers grabbed him by the middle of the tail."

But being a slippery fellow, Albert managed to wriggle out of the keeper's grasp and make a fast dive to the bottom of the lake. That ended the day's alligator hunt.

Freiheit said no attempt would be made to shoot Albert with a tranquilizer gun, for fear he would sink to the bottom of the lake and die.

July 14, 1981

Gator crew bags Albert on day 28

By FRANCES MELROSE
News Staff

Albert's 28 halcyon days of freedom came to an end at 1:30 a.m. Wednesday when he caught his nose in a noose.

The AWOL alligator has been roaming at will in the Denver Zoo Lake and City Park's Duck Lake ever since he made a clean getaway from the zoo's alligator pen nearly a month ago. The two lakes actually are one, divided by a fence.

Albert, named for the alligator in the old "Pogo" comic strip, had eluded repeated efforts to capture him. In doing so, he built a fan club of Albert watchers and Albert rooters who were sad to hear of his capture.

The agile gator made daily appearances about 12 feet from shore, paddling or lying motionless with only snout and eyes above the water. But he took off like a jet if wouldbe captors approached.

It is believed that Albert, who measures 5-foot-5, has been living on carp and catfish — and an occasional baby duck.

Albert's antics inspired buttons, a song, bumper stickers and T-shirts.

After two unsuccessful daylight attempts to capture Albert Tuesday, a zoo crew consisting of assistant director Paul Linger, head keeper Rex Williams, assistant Mike Kinsey and general curator Ed Schmitt went alligator hunting at 11 p.m. Their main weapon was a searchlight, with which they had hoped to dazzle Albert.

Linger and Schmitt went out on a limb when Albert was spotted near a corner of the island in Duck Lake. They climbed out on a tree branch over the lake above Albert, but the gator spotted them and swam off. Meanwhile, Williams and Kinsey, who were standing by in a boat, paddled after the retreating reptile.

Albert took refuge under a raft in the lake, one of his favorite hiding spots. Schmitt spotted him by directing the light through a hole in the raft.

Quickly the men erected a fence around the raft. Then they tore a board off the raft and shined the light into his eyes. Schmitt then snared him with a catchpole, fastening the noose around the alligator's snout. His jaws were bound shut to keep him from biting.

"He wriggled around a lot, but couldn't get loose," said Williams. He was too big to pull up through the hole, so we had to tear off another board."

Following his capture, Albert was placed in solitary confinement in the old grotto under sheep mountain in the zoo and was transferred to the zoo's Monkey Island, a rustic Alcatraz surrounded by a moat and high cement walls.

Escape will be virtually impossible, according to Clayton Freiheit, zoo director. "But it's a very nice place. It has grass and trees and plenty of water." The public will be able to see him there.

Seven hooded capuchin monkeys and two capybaras (large South American rodents resembling guinea pigs) will share the island with Albert, but monkeys and alligators are used to sharing habitats, Linger said.

"I understand we formerly mixed alligators and monkeys on the island," he said. "There was no trouble except that the monkeys sometimes teased the alligators."

Albert and several other alligators are on loan from the Cheyenne Mountain Zoo in Colorado Springs, but they will be returned at the end of summer because the Denver Zoo has no winter accommodations for them.

"We had to capture Albert before cold weather set in or he would have died," said Freiheit.

Albert's only comment is a slow, malicious hiss delivered at any approaching zoo keeper.

Wednesday night's touted candlelight vigil at City Park Duck Lake was quiet and dark. Nobody showed up.

Fans of Albert had announced plans for the vigil to mourn the end of Albert's freedom.

Perhaps it was the clouds that threatened to rain on Albert's somber party. Or perhaps his fans were seeking a new cause to champion. Stardom is a fleeting thing.

July 16, 1981

(Fig. 11.2 continues on page 160.)

Fig. 11.2. — *Continued*

Lonely Albert gets a gator aide

Albert the alligator, who this summer became a celebrity, has a friend on Monkey Island in the Denver Zoo.

Since his recapture on July 15 after 28 days of freedom in City Park's Duck Lake, the young 5-foot-5 alligator has been confined to the rustic Alcatraz of the monkey habitat, surrounded by a moat and high cement walls, where escape is virtually impossible. Albert's only companions there have been seven capuchin monkeys and a pair of capybaras, large South American rodents.

The rest of the zoo's alligators, who knew better than to try to escape, have remained in the alligator pen. Albert, who was named for the alligator in the old Pogo comic strip, has been without associates of his own kind for several weeks. But on Wednesday he got a companion.

A Cheyenne couple who wished to remain anonymous arrived at the zoo with an alligator, which has been their household pet for 11 years. He or she — with alligators it is hard to tell — outgrew his or her surroundings and a transfer to the zoo seemed the only answer.

"I didn't care to test this one's athletic ability," said the zoo director, Clayton Freiheit. "We just started out with it on the island with Albert."

On Thursday the two gators were keeping a wary distance from one another, but they may strike up a friendship in a few days, zoo personnel said.

July 28, 1981

- Read Peter Lippman's *The Great Escape or the Sewer Story*. List the things you liked about the story and the things that surprised you. Make lists of things that were factual and things that were fantasy.

- Ask your librarian to help you find other stories about these large reptiles. How are the stories alike? How are they different?

- Make a fact book about alligators. Include pictures of alligators and things made from alligator hides.

- Investigate the genre of alphabet books and make a list of how many use *alligator* to illustrate the letter *A*. Create an alphabet book that includes endangered species.

Alligators as Symbols

- A line of sportswear with an alligator symbol became very fashionable at one time. Some teen-agers cut the alligator logos off old clothing and appliqued them to decorate socks, pants, notebooks, bumper stickers, tote bags, and other objects. What fashion statements featuring alligators can you think of to add to this list?

NOTES

1. Jan Harold Brunvand, *The Vanishing Hitchhiker* (New York: Norton, 1981).

2. *New York Times*, February 10, 1935.

RESOURCE BIBLIOGRAPHY

Brunvand, Jan Harold. *The Vanishing Hitchhiker*. New York: Norton, 1981.
   The author has collected the best examples of the various legends and "urban folklore" from all over the United States and Canada and shows how the stories have been adapted to changes in locale and popular lifestyles over the years.

George, Jean Craighead. *The Moon of the Alligator*. Illustrated by Michael Rothman. New York: HarperCollins, 1991.
   The author describes an alligator's desperate search for food in the Florida Everglades during the month of October.

Ling, Mary. *Amazing Crocodiles and Reptiles*. New York: Knopf, 1991.
   The habits, diet, and characteristics of several kinds of crocodiles, alligators, turtles, snakes, and lizards are detailed in text and photographs.

Lippman, Peter. *The Great Escape or the Sewer Story*. New York: Golden Press, 1973.
   Lippman chronicles how New York City's sewer alligators return to the Florida swamps by disguising themselves as tourists and chartering a flight from which they bail out over the wetlands.

McCarthy, Colin. *Eyewitness Books: Reptile*. New York: Knopf, 1991.
    Photographs and text depict the many kinds of reptiles, their similarities and differences, their habitats, and their behavior. Beautiful photographs complement the interesting textual information.

Scott, Jack Denton. *Alligator*. Illustrated with photographs by Ozzie Sweet. New York: Putnam, 1984.
    The author discusses characteristics that have enabled some species to flourish.

Shaw, Evelyn. *Alligator*. Illustrated by Frances Zweifel. New York: Harper, 1972.
    This picture book describes an alligator's life cycle in narrative form with no anthropomorphism.

Resource Information

When you need to find out more information about endangered animals and what is being done to preserve and protect them, contact the following groups.

The Conservation Foundation
1717 Massachusetts Avenue, N.W.
Washington, DC 20036

Council on Economic Priorities
456 Greenwich Street
New York, NY 10013

Defenders of Wildlife
2000 N Street, N.W.
Washington, DC 20036

Environmental Action, Inc.
1346 Connecticut Avenue, N.W.
Room 731
Washington, DC 20036

Environmental Defense Fund, Inc.
162 Old Town Road
East Setauket, NY 11733

Friends of the Earth
529 Commercial Street
San Francisco, CA 94111

Greenpeace USA
1436 U Street
Washington, DC 20009

League of Women Voters of the U.S.
1730 M Street, N.W.
Washington, DC 20036

National Audubon Society
950 Third Avenue
New York, NY 10022

National Parks and Conservation
    Association
1701 18th Street, N.W.
Washington, DC 20009

National Wildlife Federation
1400 16th Street, N.W.
Washington, DC 20036

Natural Resources Council of
    America
1025 Connecticut Avenue, N.W.
Suite 911
Washington, DC 20036

Natural Resources Defense Council
40 West 20th Street
New York, NY 10011

The Nature Conservancy
1815 North Lynn Street
Arlington, VA 22209

Scientists' Institute for Public
    Information
438 North Skinker
St. Louis, MO 63130

Sierra Club
Public Affairs Department
730 Polk Street
San Francisco, CA 94109

The Wilderness Society
900 17th Street, N.W.
Washington, DC 20006

Wilderness Watch
P.O. Box 3184
Green Bay, WI 54303

Wildlife Management Institute
709 Wire Building
Washington, DC 20005

World Wildlife Fund/Conservation
    Foundation
1250 24th Street, N.W.
Suite 400
Washington, DC 20037

For a more extensive listing of conservation organizations, see *The Conservation Directory* (Washington, D.C.: National Wildlife Federation, 1989, 1991). Also contact state agencies such as your state Division of Wildlife.

Suggested Readings

Adoff, Arnold. *Birds*. Illustrated by Howell Troy. New York: Harper-Collins/Lippincott, 1982.

Armour, Richard. *Strange Monsters of the Sea*. Illustrated by Paul Galdone. New York: McGraw-Hill, 1979.

Arnold, Caroline. *Snake*. New York: Morrow, 1991.

Balog, James. *Survivors: A New Vision of Endangered Wildlife*. New York: Abrams, 1990.

Banks, Martin. *Endangered Wildlife*. Vero Beach, Fla.: Rourke Publishers, 1988.

Bateman, Robert. *Robert Bateman: An Artist in Nature*. New York: Random House, 1990.

Berrill, Jacquelyn. *Wonders of Animal Migration*. New York: Dodd Mead, 1964.

Bonners, Susan. *Panda*. New York: Delacorte Press, 1978.

Braun, Bertel. *Animals: The Strange and Exciting Stories of Their Lives*. Silver Springs, Md.: American Heritage Press, 1970.

Brooks, Bruce. *Predator!* New York: Farrar, Straus & Giroux, 1991.

Brower, Kenneth. *One Earth*. New York: Collins, 1990.

Buckles, Mary Parker. *Animals of the World*. New York: Grossett & Dunlap, 1978.

Burton, Jane. *The Color Nature Library; Baby Animals*. United Kingdom: Crescent Books, 1977.

Burton, John. *Close to Extinction*. New York: Gloucester Press, 1988.

Carle, Eric. *Animals, Animals*. New York: Philomel, 1989.

Carrington, Richard. *The Mammals*. Westwood, N.J.: Time-Life, 1969.

Carter, Anne. *Birds, Beasts and Fishes*. Illustrated by Reg Cartwright. New York: Macmillan, 1991.

Civarcli, Anne, and Cathy Kilpatrick. *How Animals Live*. London: Usborne, 1976.

Climo, Shirley. *King of the Birds*. New York: Harper Trophy, 1991.

Cole, William. *An Arkful of Animals: Poems for the Very Young*. Illustrated by Lynn Munsinger. Boston: Houghton, 1978.

Collins, Mark. *The Last Rain Forests: A World Conservation Atlas*. New York: Oxford, 1990.

Cosgrove, Margaret. *Wintertime for Animals*. New York: Dodd Mead, 1975.

Cowcher, Helen. *Rain Forest*. New York: Farrar, Straus & Giroux Sunburst Book, 1991.

Crutchins, Judy. *The Crocodile and the Crane*. New York: Morrow, 1986.

Dahl, Roald. *The Enormous Crocodile*. New York: Knopf, 1978.

Daniel, Mark, ed. *A Child's Treasury of Animal Verse*. New York: Dial, 1989.

Darling, Kathy. *Walrus on Location*. Photographs by Tara Darling. New York: Lothrop, Lee & Shepard, 1991.

Debnam, Betty. "Endangered Species." *The Mini Page*. Universal Press Syndicate, March 6, 1991.

Dorros, Arthur. *Animal Tracks*. New York: Scholastic, 1991.

Earle, Olive L. *Paws, Hoofs, and Flippers*. New York: Morrow, 1954.

Epple, Ann Orth. *The Look Alikes*. New York: St. Martin's Press, 1971.

Esbensen, Barbara Juster. *Tiger with Wings: The Great Horned Owl*. Illustrated by Mary Barrett Brown. New York: Orchard, 1991.

Faber, Doris, and Harold Faber. *Nature and the Environment Great Lives*. New York: Scribner's, 1991.

Few, Roger. *Macmillan Animal Encyclopedia for Children*. New York: Macmillan, 1991.

Fleischman, Paul. *I Am Phoenix: Poems for Two Voices*. Illustrated by Ken Nutt. New York: HarperCollins, 1985.

Ford, Barbara. *Wildlife Rescue*. Morton Grove, Ill.: Albert Whitman, 1987.

Freedman, Russell. *Hanging On: How Animals Carry Their Young*. New York: Holiday House, 1977.

———. *Tooth and Claw*. New York: Holiday House, 1980.

Gardner, John C. *A Child's Bestiary*. New York: Knopf, 1977.

Gerstenfeld, Sheldon L. *Zoo Clues (Making the Most of Your Visit to the Zoo)*. Illustrated by Eldon C. Doty. New York: Viking, 1991.

Gove, Doris. *A Water Snake's Year*. Illustrated by Beverly Duncan. New York: Atheneum, 1991.

Graham, Ada, and Frank Graham. *Whale Watch*. New York: Delacorte, 1945, 1975.

Graves, Eleanor, ed. *Birds of Sea, Shore, and Stream*. Westwood, N.J.: Time-Life, 1976.

Gray, Robert. *Children of the Ark: The Rescue of the World's Vanishing Wildlife*. New York: Scholastic, 1973.

Gross, Ruth. *Pandas*. New York: Scholastic, 1972.

Halmi, Robert. *In the Wilds of Africa*. New York: Four Winds Press, 1971.

Harris, Lorle. *Biography of a Whooping Crane*. New York: Putnam, 1977.

Hefter, Richard, and Martin Moskof. *The Endangered Wildlife Shufflebook*. New York: Museum of Modern Art, 1991.

Hodges, Margaret. *Brother Francis and the Friendly Beasts*. Illustrated by Ted Lewin. New York: Scribner's, 1991.

Hoffmeister, Donald. *Zoo Animals*. New York: Golden Press, 1967.

Hooper, Patricia. *A Bundle of Beasts*. Illustrated by Mark Steele. Boston: Houghton Mifflin, 1987.

Horowitz, Ruth. *Bat Time*. Illustrated by Susan Avishai. New York: Four Winds Press, 1991.

Hyde, Margaret. *Animal Clocks and Compasses*. New York: McGraw-Hill, 1960.

Jeffers, Susan. *Brother Eagle, Sister Sky*. New York: Dial, 1991.

Johnston, Ginny. *Slippery Babies*. Illustrated by Judy Cutchins. New York: Morrow, 1991.

Kennedy, Michael. *Australia's Endangered Species*. Englewood Cliffs, N.J.: Prentice-Hall, 1990.

LaBonte, Gail. *The Arctic Fox*. New York: Dillon, 1989.

Lane, Frank W. *Zoo Animals*. United Kingdom: Crescent Books, 1972.

Lear, Edward. *The Scroobious Pip*. Illustrated by Nancy Ekholm Burkert. New York: Harper & Row Junior Books, 1968; HarperCollins/Trophy, 1987.

Lerner, Carol. *A Desert Year*. New York: Morrow, 1991.

Lovell, Sarah. *Extremely Weird Bats*. Santa Fe, N. Mex.: John Muir Publications, 1991.

Lyons, Beth. *Book of Endangered Species*. Illustrated by Ken Maestas. Denver, Colo.: Earthbooks, 1991.

Mahey, Margaret. *The Girl with the Green Ear*. Illustrated by Shirley Hughes. New York: Knopf, 1992.

Mallory, Kenneth. *Rescue of the Stranded Whales*. New York: Simon & Schuster, 1989.

Manning, Linda. *Animal Hours*. Illustrated by Vlasta van Kampen. New York: Oxford, 1990.

Marsh, James. *Bizarre Birds and Beasts*. New York: Dial, 1991.

Martin, Louise. *Elephants*. Vero Beach, Fla.: Rourke Publishers, 1988.

———. *Tigers*. Vero Beach, Fla.: Rourke Publishers, 1988.

Mason, George. *Animal Sounds*. New York: Morrow, 1948, 1972.

Matthews, Downs. *Polar Bear Cubs*. Photographs by Dan Guravich. New York: Simon & Schuster, 1989.

May, John. *The Greenpeace Book of Dolphins*. New York: Sterling, 1990.

Mazer, Anne. *The Salamander Room*. Illustrated by Steve Johnson. New York: Knopf, 1991.

McCoy, J. J. *The Plight of the Whales*. New York: Watts, 1989.

McGovern, Ann, and Eugenie Clark. *The Desert Beneath the Sea*. Illustrated by Craig Phillips. New York: Scholastic, 1991.

Morris, Desmond. *Animalwatching*. New York: Crown, 1990.

Ommanney, F. D. *The Fishes*. Westwood, N.J.: Time-Life, 1968.

Parker, Steve. *Pond and River*. New York: Knopf, 1988.

Peterson, Scott K. *Wing It! Riddles about Birds*. Illustrated by Susan Slattery Burke. Minneapolis, Minn.: Lerner, 1991.

Prelutsky, Jack. *Zoo Doings: Animal Poems*. Illustrated by Paul O. Zelinsky. New York: Greenwillow, 1983.

Pringle, Laurence. *Living Treasure: Saving Earth's Threatened Biodiversity*. Illustrated by Irene Brady. New York: Morrow, 1991.

Rau, Margaret. *The Giant Panda at Home*. New York: Knopf, 1977.

Russell, William F. *Animal Families of the Wild*. (A read-aloud collection of animal literature.) Illustrated by John Butler. New York: Random House, 1990.

Selsam, Millicent. *How the Animals Eat*. Illustrated by Helen Ludwig. New York: W. R. Scott, 1955.

_____. *The Language of Animals*. New York: Morrow, 1962.

Silverberg, Robert. *The Awk, the Dodo, and the Oryx: Vanished and Vanishing Creatures*. New York: Crowell, 1977.

Simon, Paul. *At the Zoo*. Illustrated by Valerie Michaut. New York: Doubleday, 1991.

Singer, Marilyn. *Turtle in July*. Illustrated by Jerry Pinkney. New York: Macmillan, 1989.

Sitwell, Sacheverell. *Fine Bird Books, 1700-1900*. Boston: Atlantic Monthly Press, 1990.

Tarboton, Warwick. *African Birds of Prey*. Ithaca, N.Y.: Cornell University Press, 1990.

Taylor, Barbara. *The Animals Atlas*. New York: Knopf, 1991.

Turner, Tom. *Wild by Law*. San Francisco, Calif.: Sierra Club, 1990.

Waters, John F. *Watching Whales*. New York: Cobblehill/Dutton, 1991.

Wegen, Ron. *Where Can the Animals Go*. New York: Greenwillow, 1978.

Yolen, Jane. *Bird Watch*. Illustrated by Ted Lewin. New York: Philomel, 1990.

Zim, Herbert. *The Great Whales*. New York: Morrow, 1951.

_____. *Mammals: Guide to Familiar American Species*. New York: Golden Press, 1964.

Index

About the Authors

Glenn McGlathery and Norma Livo joined the education faculty of the University of Colorado at Denver in the fall of 1968 and have worked together on countless activities, from mundane academic meetings to highly charged storytelling conferences. Both served on PROJECT WILD writing teams. Although they have undertaken many and varied projects jointly, this is their first collaboration on a book.

Glenn McGlathery received his B.A. in English at Texas Wesleyan College in Forth Worth and the M.Ed. and Ph.D. in science education from the University of Texas at Austin. He taught in public schools in Texas and at the University of Texas in Austin. He has been a professor of science education at the University of Colorado at Denver since 1968. He is married, the father of two, and the grandfather of four. He and Larry Malone wrote *Tons of Scientifically Provocative and Socially Acceptable Things to Do with Balloons under the Guise of Teaching Science*.

Norma J. Livo received her B.S., M.Ed., and Ed.D. from the University of Pittsburgh, Pennsylvania. She has taught at the elementary and secondary levels and has been a professor of education at the University of Colorado at Denver since 1968. She is the mother of four children and the grandmother of five. Stories and storytelling are important to her in both her professional and personal life.